Botanica Erotica

Botanica Erotica

Arousing
Body, Mind, and Spirit

Diana De Luca

Healing Arts Press
Rochester, Vermont

Healing Arts Press
One Park Street
Rochester, Vermont 05767
www.InnerTraditions.com

Note to the reader: This book is intended as an informational guide. The remedies, approaches, and techniques described herein are meant to supplement, and not to be a substitute for, professional medical care or treatment. They should not be used to treat a serious ailment without prior consultation with a qualified health-care professional.

Library of Congress Cataloging-in-Publication Data
De Luca, Diana, 1957–
    Botanica erotica : arousing body, mind, and spirit / Diana De Luca.
       p.   cm.
    Includes index.
    ISBN 0-89281-790-9 (hardback : alk. paper)
    1. Sexual excitement. 2. Aphrodisiacs. 3. Bathing customs. I. Title.
HQ25.D4   1998   98-20823
613.9'6—dc21   CIP

Printed and bound in the United States

10 9 8 7 6 5 4 3 2 1

Text design and layout by Kristin Camp
This book was typeset in Caslon with Shelley Volante and Bernhard Modern as the display typefaces

Frontispiece: Sir Lawrence Alma-Tadema, *Welcome Footsteps,* 1883. Oil on canvas. Private collection.

Healing Arts Press is a division of Inner Traditions International

Acknowledgment is made for permission to quote from "In Praise of Vanilla," from *A Natural History of the Senses,* © 1990 by Diane Ackerman, reprinted with permission of Random House, Inc.

Acknowledgment is made for permission to reproduce the following photographs:
Page 56: Photograph by Max Meyers.
Pages 68, 72, 80, 100: Photographs by Hari Meyers.
Page 105: *Plums* by Vincent Dame (1946–1995). Glazed ceramics, height 4.5 cm. Galerie Vignet, Amsterdam.
    Photograph by Vincent Dame. Reproduced with permission of Remus Thei Dame.
Page 112: Photograph of Shiva lingam garlanded with offering flowers and substances, Bengal, by Nik Douglas.
    Reproduced with permission of Nik Douglas.

Acknowledgments

I would like to gratefully acknowledge and thank my parents Sam and Nel De Luca, my sisters Doreen and Debra, my son Nic, and my Sicilian grandparents and ancestors for their love and support. Special thanks to David Hoffmann for the guidance, support, and inspiration to write this book. Thank you to herbalists and fellow Garlic Queens: Rosemary, Mindy, Brigitte, and Kathi for your inspiration, friendship, and herbal wisdom. I would like to thank my friends and extended family for their love and support including: Olga, Lois, Shayna, Aalan, Theresa and Alan, Scarlett, Dan, Isis, Vivien, Karen, Kelly, Pablo, Hari, Heather, Phyllis, Dae, Gina, and my sisters and brothers of the Hahbi `Ru Music and Dance Ensemble. Thank you to Mary Elder Jacobsen for her excellent help as editor and Kristin Camp for design.

I would also like to acknowledge all the women and men who have attended my herbal classes and workshops throughout the years.

Live juicy! Love juicy!

May your body be blessed.
May you realize that your body is a faithful and beautiful friend of your
    soul.
May you recognize that your senses are sacred thresholds.
May you realize that holiness is mindful gazing, mindful feeling, mindful
    listening, and mindful touching.
May your senses always enable you to celebrate the universe and the
    mystery and possibilities in your presence here.
May Eros bless you.
May your senses gather you and bring you home.

Old Celtic Blessing

Contents

Four
Aphrodisiac Foods and Voluptuous Vittles 52

Five

Libidinous Libations:
Thirst-Quenching, Revitalizing, and Refreshing Beverages 77

Six

Beauty and the Bath: Lascivious Lavage   92

Seven

Sensual Body Work   104

Foreword

A unique book written by a wonderful herbalist who freely shares her adeptness in the diverse ways of using herbs, *Botanica Erotica* blends real herbalism with a joyful affirmation of sensuality, one that can come only when real experience blends with the consciousness of a green wise woman. The result is a fun and empowering book, offering a cornucopia of pleasure to all who read it.

The medieval herbalist and mystic Hildegard von Bingen talks of *viriditas*, "the greening power." By "greening power," I interpret her to mean a vital energy that is life, the spirit of the planet, the divine in form, that heals and transforms humanity. The healing offered so abundantly and freely by our plant relatives is indeed a greening of the human condition, pointing to the reality of a new springtime. Herbalism can be a very special doorway into our reconnection with nature. The embrace of the sensual, an affirmation of the body, and the simple enjoyment of its pleasures are yet another. So how timely for *Botanica Erotica* to blend the two—and how much fun!

David Hoffmann
Sebastopol, California

Before a Mirror, Robert Barrett
Browning, 1846–1912.

Introduction

Humankind has forever been in search of the perfect aphrodisiac. From ancient to modern times almost no culture, primitive or civilized, has been without its cornucopia of love foods. The term *aphrodisiac*, as we know it, comes from classical Greece and stems from Aphrodite, the Greek goddess of love. Aphrodisiacs are substances that excite sexual desire or enhance sexual performance. They include—in addition to those substances taken internally—visual, aural, tactile, and olfactory stimulants; in short, *anything* that inspires sensuality.

For most people there is nothing quite like a partner who is warm, nurturing, communicative, and willing to explore options that fit and work for both partners. Each person has his or her own special needs and desires around being pleasured. Communicating to find out what is really pleasing and what turns each person on and then making sure that those needs and desires are included in lovemaking can certainly be one of the best aphrodisiacs possible.

As an herbalist in my community since 1980 I have had the privilege and pleasure of

giving herbal workshops around the United States and Canada. In the course of my travels many women and men have approached me with the common and quietly whispered question, "Do you have something, you know, ahem, herbs for the bedroom?" It was such a regular occurrence that I began to research and investigate collections of herbal books, many out of print, that described the foods, plants, and herbs used throughout antiquity as aphrodisiacs. There are many good books on the market that provide detailed descriptions of the herbal world; however, I caution the reader to go carefully. There are books, for example, that give historical accounts of herbs as aphrodisiacs but do not give information on dosage or contraindications. This leaves the reader to experiment without proper knowledge of the toxicity of certain plants. In *Botanica Erotica* I prefer to focus on the tonic and nourishing effects and do not recommend experimentation with potentially dangerous plants.

I have compiled this book to inspire and

French postcard, photograph, 1920s.

guide you, not only to create and personalize the recipes but, in addition, to help yourself and your lover to remain healthy, as well as juicy!

Probably the earliest recorded mention of aphrodisiacs comes from undated Egyptian medical papyri believed to be from the Middle Kingdom, which flourished between 2200–1700 B.C.E. Aphrodisiacs are mentioned in the Bible and many of the world's sacred books. Ancient literature is filled with glowing accounts of aphrodisiac foods. By the time of the Golden Age of Greece, their use was fairly commonplace. The Romans were also intimately familiar with the art of culinary seduction. Aphrodisiac lore passed from the Roman to the early Christian era, through the Middle Ages and the Renaissance, and into modern times. I have included some of these antique aphrodisiacs for their historical interest at the end of the book.

The list of aphrodisiac foods ranges from the exotic to the commonplace. Even such unromantic items as the potato and the bean were once considered powerful love stimulants. The idea that a potato in the dining room can lead to a frolic in the bedroom may not be as ridiculous as it sounds.

I present some of my favorite aphrodisiacs with stories and recipes, and my hope is that they will inspire your sensual self to come out and play and celebrate life. There is so much grief, sorrow, and pain in this world. Whenever we allow ourselves to experience pleasure, smell wonderful smells, make juicy love, enjoy a red and purple sunset, it heals us. As we allow pleasure into our lives, the Earth, too, feels pleasure, and we are simultaneously healed.

Chapter 1

Love Gods and Goddesses:
A Pantheon of Sensuality

Gods and goddesses of erotic love have inspired humans since antiquity with their awesome presence through dance and song, music and food, grapes and roses, ecstatic celebrations and feasts to honor sacred sensuality and celebrate life. Each culture has had their own god or goddess that was invoked to inspire sensuality and love.

For ages female sexuality was embodied by courtesans and prostitutes. These women were well educated and held in high esteem in the community. Many of them lived, worked, danced, played music, taught, and gardened at the temple. They served their community, those who came to the temple to pay respect to the goddess of love and ask for her blessing upon their lives, family, and food. They brought gold coins as offerings, and no amount of payment was ever turned down. Each woman of the community did her time at the temple in honor and respect of the high goddess. The consecrated priestesses in the temple were also known as sacred prostitutes and initiated into the highest ranks of sacred sexuality and pleasure. The meaning of the word *prostitute* was

"one who stood on behalf of" or represented the great goddess. From the goddess, feminine power flowed through the spiritually receptive ancient temple prostitute while she passionately celebrated her own beauty and sexuality.

Capitoline Aphrodite, sculpture.

Aphrodite

Aphrodite, born from the foam of the sea, is well known as the Greek goddess of love, and is often seen crowned in spring blossoms. She is associated with desire, seduction, sexual love, and ecstasy. Aphrodite wore a magic girdle that caused those who saw her to fall in love with her immediately. The dove and the dolphin, apples, roses, lilies, fennel, opium poppies, pomegranates, myrrh, cinnamon, and myrtle are sacred to her. Her temples were erected throughout Greece, Turkey, and the Mediterranean islands, including Sicily and Cyprus. She was honored with gifts of roses, fruits, fragrant plants, and beautiful birds. In summer's heat her passion is sweet, she laughs from leafy bowers.

It is very important for women to feel the touch of the goddess of love, for sensual enjoyment transforms our attitudes toward ourselves, others, and life in general, bringing renewed beauty, vitality, and liveliness.

Apsaras

The Apsaras were originally human women, priestesses of the sacred sexual rites in twelfth-century Asia, who were also known as the Daughters of Pleasure. These women were educated and known for their intellect. They played music among the fig trees and took as many lovers, both human and divine, as they pleased. They wore magnificent headdresses and beautiful, sensual garments. They adorned themselves with aromatic flowers as they danced and celebrated life.

The Many-Breasted Artemis or Diana of Ephesus

This ancient goddess of fertility, sexuality, and nourishment was worshiped in the Near East and Greece, especially in Anatolia. She stands tall and has an abundance of breasts; the many layers of her skirt represent the animal, plant, and mineral kingdoms, which are sacred to her.

Cleopatra

Cleopatra was born in Greece in 60 B.C.E. and died in 30 B.C.E. At eighteen she became the famous queen of Egypt. She was much skilled in the art of love and seduction; her beauty and charm were like no other's. She was known as the living goddess. The sails of her boat were

perfumed with roses and incense to announce her arrival, but her entrance to the palace in Alexandria was in an oriental carpet, which was unrolled to reveal the beautiful young queen. Cleopatra teaches us about setting the mood or atmosphere for a passionate seduction by including beautiful robes, aromatic essences, rich colors, and a sensuous food feast. Neroli, oil of orange blossoms, is a haunting fragrance much loved by Cleopatra. She can inspire us to remember to pamper ourselves, as she often did by bathing in milk with roses and having her body lavishly massaged with olive or sesame oil scented with flowers and spices. She knew how to make the most of clothing, perfumes, and jewels. Alexandrian women loved to make perfumes, unguents, scented oils, and eye makeup, and Cleopatra is said to have written a treatise on cosmetics. She imported exquisite Chinese silks, whose close weave was unthreaded to produce a diaphanous look, allowing her breasts to show through. Her temple palace was rich with golds, deep purples, and brilliant magenta. As Plutarch described her

The Ephesian Artemis, sculpture. Mansell Collection.

in his *Life of Antony*, she came sailing up the river Cydnus, in

> a barge with gilded stern and sails of purple, while oars of silver beat time to the music of flutes and fifes and harps. She herself lay all along under a canopy of cloth of gold, dressed as Venus in a picture, and beautiful young boys, like painted Cupids, stood on each side to fan her. Her maids were dressed like sea nymphs and graces, some steering at the rudder, some working at the ropes. The perfumes diffused themselves from the vessel to the shore.

Her seductiveness lay not only in her smooth, charming voice, but in her renowned vivacity and intelligence.

Horae

Horae is the Greek word signifying a period of time like the seasons of the year or hours of the day. Aphrodite's celestial nymphs inspired

Gustave Moreau, *Cleopatra.* c. 1887. Watercolor.

earthly horae (harlot-priestesses) to train men in the sexual mysteries. They mellowed the behavior of men.

These priestesses kept the hours at the temple, like the vestal virgins who kept the sacred hearthfire burning continuously. They symbolized the blossoming of the flowers in spring and the ripening of fruit in summer.

Ishtar-Inanna

In Babylonian times, the goddess Ishtar was known as the Queen of Heaven. She stood poised, holding her breasts forward as an offering, and was also known as Inanna in ancient Sumeria. Her love poems to her beloved consort Dumuzi reveal potent sacred eroticism. She rejoiced in her own sexuality and opened the portals of heaven through her priestesses. She appears in the Bible as Anath, Ashtoreth, or Asherah, and as Astarte and Mari in the Near East. She was also known as The Light of the World, The Great Whore, Mother of Harlots, and Babylon the Great. She was represented by her sacred prostitute-priestesses, known as Ishtaritu or Joy Maidens, who, through sexual union, bestowed her divine power on those who

sought her blessings. All acts of love and pleasure were her rituals.

Mary Magdalene

Mary Magdalene was a sacred harlot and a funerary priestess. She was also known as The Woman Who Knew All and The Woman with the Alabaster Jar. Magdalene means *she of the temple tower*. The magdalene and her women, priestesses of the temple, financially supported Jesus and the apostles. The magdalene anointed

*I am the first
and the last.
I am the honored one
and the scorned one.
I am the whore,
and the holy one.*

Marjorie Malvern,
Venus in Sackcloth

her beloved Christ with a fragrant unguent she made from precious oils, believed to include the fragrant herb spikenard and olive oil. She was an herbalist who mixed healing balms and remedies from her temple gardens, using many of the same plants that can be found in our own gardens, including rosemary and thyme.

A sacred brothel in Rome later was established by Pope Julius II to support the Holy Sisters of the Order of St. Mary Magdalene, also known as the magdalenes, or sacred whores. It was publicly announced that anyone who married one of them would be blessed and specially praised in heaven.

I found God within myself, and I loved her. I loved her fiercely.
Ntozake Shange

One of the church ceremonies my very loving Sicilian-American family participated in as devoted Catholics was the confirmation ceremony. This ceremony was enacted as a way of acknowledging and confirming one's faith in the church. At this time, one must choose the name of a saint whose attributes are personally inspiring, a name the bishop must approve. At the age of thirteen, during my confirmation ceremony, I proudly announced that I had chosen Mary Magdalene as my patroness saint. The bishop blundered and fumbled in dismay and confusion and, upon recovering himself, instantly scolded me, announcing that the Catholic church did not recognize Mary Magdalene as a saint. I turned around, ready to exit, despite the pleading eyes of my mother, who begged me to stay. I could read her lips saying, "Saint Francis!" I decided to stay in order not to cause any more embarrassment. I then chose Saint Francis to appease the onlookers, as I was born on his feast day and he was commonly associated with his special love of gardens and animals. But in my heart of hearts it was Mary Magdalene I chose that day.

My work is in honor of Mary Magdalene, my patroness saint.

Mae West, 1933 film still. Museum of Modern Art, New York.

Mae West

A more contemporary sex goddess, Mae West was famous for her excitable, humorous femme-fatale persona and made a definitely political sexual declaration by her perception of the subject. An amusing entertainer, she was the most highly paid woman in Hollywood during the height of her career in the 1930s.

Oshun

Honey is the favorite offering to this African goddess of love and river goddess of fertility. She is said to smooth herself with honey and wear yellow scarves around her waist and peacock feathers in her hair as her beautiful breasts glimmer in the sun. Bells and fans, water animals, and plants are sacred to her. She is sometimes depicted as a double-tailed mermaid. She knows secrets by divination and uses seashells to read the future.

Sappho

Sappho, born around 600 B.C.E., was the only female lyricist of antiquity whose work has come down to our age. She lived most of her life on the Greek island of Lesbos. The archetypal lesbian, she wrote erotic poetry and songs openly.

Venus

A lover of laughter, Venus was a Roman love goddess recognized for her irresistible charm. We see her in the sky each night as Venus the evening star. *Star light, star bright, first star I see tonight, I wish I may, I wish I might, have the wish I wish tonight.* Temples were dedicated to her, schools of instruction in sexual techniques taught by *Venerii,* or harlot-priestesses. She is associated with the Greek goddess Aphrodite.

Animal and Plant Gods of Love and Ecstasy

Love gods have appeared throughout history as beneficent and sacred bulls, rams, lions, tigers, panthers, goats, snakes, and stags. Honoring the wisdom of plants and nature, the Green Man or god of the greenwood is portrayed with a beautiful leafy face and beard, a botanical god symbolizing man's wild, passionate nature.

Stone carvings have been found over doorways throughout the Celtic countries, symbolizing man's interaction with the sacredness of all Mother Nature.

Cernunnos was the Celtic horned god and stag of the forest and was the consort of the moon

---

William Bouguereau, *La Naissance de Vénus,* 1879. Oil on canvas. Musée d'Orsay, Paris.

goddess. He was half man and half stag, wearing antlers and sporting his virility as he protected and honored nature and the greenwoods.

Bull gods, half man and half bull, have long been noted for their connection with celestial and earthly influences. Among them are Zeus and Dionysus in Greece, Minos the Minotaur from Crete, Nandi the joyous bull of Shiva in India, Cernunnos the Celtic horned god, and Apis the Egyptian bull-god king. The bull represented the male principle of fertility sharing his sexual favors and energy among female devotees and initiates.

Dionysus

In Greek mythology, Dionysus's totem was a panther and he carried a phallic scepter topped with a pinecone. Dionysus is also identified with Bacchus, Adonis, and Pan. Erotic, lusty bacchanalian festivals in honor of the god of the grape harvest and the drinking of the sacred wine were celebrated with wild, frenzied danc-

ing. Beautiful women were clad in flowing gowns with leopard skins tied to their bodies, while men wore garlands of grapevines with the grapes dangling around their faces. The food,

Dionysus, bas-relief from Herculaneum. National Museum, Naples.

the drink, the music, and the dancing carried on for days, since this harvest festival was the greatest of the year and celebrated the best of life.

Eros

Eros symbolizes our deepest sensual, sexual, erotic selves. In Roman mythology Eros was represented as a beautiful, androgynous youth who was transformed into the god of love; his function was to seduce all creatures, male and female. Watch what you wish for—Eros and Cupid have been known to sneak up unexpectedly while the spring flowers are blossoming.

Eros is our deepest internal wellspring of passion, honoring both love and lust. Eros is born of Mother Nature, *Mamma Natura* in Italian.

Pan

Pan is one of the oldest of Greek gods. He was also known as the king of satyrs, hoofed and horned, half man and half goat. Pan sniffs the fresh spring air for his favorite sylvan pasttime, coupling with water nymphs by the lake.

The god or goddess of love lives within each and every one of us and it is a matter of luring him or her out with a feast for the senses.

Christianity gave Eros poison to drink, he did not die of it, but degenerated into a vice.

Nietzsche

Chapter 2

Creating a Love Ceremony

An Invitation to a Pleasure Feast for the Senses!

It is important to take time out of the ordinary, everyday routine to create a nurturing, sensual space. This can be done in different ways. You can put together your own "pleasure temple"— a comfortable space indoors or out where you can feel free to express your sensuality. Why not have a picnic on your bed? Or a rendezvous in your living room for midnight at the oasis, or a moon-bathing fruit feast on a warm summer's eve?

Attitude, atmosphere, and power of sug-

gestion are of primary importance when setting the mood. You can start delighting the senses by including sight, sound, smell, taste, and touch in your pleasuring. Turn your life into a garden of sensual delights.

Take a few minutes to arrange candles and flowers, create a circle of rose petals, or lay a trail of flower petals leading to the boudoir or

Andreas Groll, *Pan and the Nymphs,* 1897. Oil on canvas. Private collection.

table laden with goodies. You may wish to select special sensuous clothing, something to attract, arouse, or enhance certain features, perhaps using diaphanous fabrics and silks.

Music can soothe the savage beast and it can also arouse the sensual creature. Sounds can be a great inspiration and can include the *yums* and *aaahhhs* of eating as well as the moans, groans, grunts, and gasps of primitive passion. Try reading or sharing erotic stories

Illusion is the first of all pleasures.
Oscar Wilde

and poems. Plan a passion picnic outdoors, where you can be inspired by a babbling brook, ocean waves, or any of the wondrous sounds of nature in a forest. Speak to your lover in an arousing manner.

Touch is the ultimate sensual and sexual sensation. You can produce pleasurable tactile sensations with soft velvety fabric, by brushing succulent silk across naked nipples, or by tantalizing, teasing, and tickling with a feather or an artist's paintbrush. The erogenous zones are the regions of the body that experience the most sensual pleasure and sexual stimulation when touched—not only the genital area, but the lips, the neck, the ears, the nipples, the hands and fingers, the inner thighs, the breasts, and the base of the spine.

As we open our hearts to the sacred erotic dimensions within and honor our sexuality, we are nourished and healed on a deep level. Give yourself permission to celebrate your sensuality in a way that tantalizes you and awakens all of your senses!

Awaken to the love goddess or love god within. Open your heart to the earth's energy through the "souls" of your feet, breathe in life and passion. Remember that you are the source of your own pleasure. Celebrate life and the sacred erotic!

Creating the Mood and Spicing Up the Atmosphere

You may want to send a special someone an invitation to share the luscious physical expression of the celebration of your sensuality through a pleasure feast for the senses. Try a written invitation, for example:

You are invited to spend the evening with the Love Goddess Herself! Let's meet in the living room at midnight for a passionate picnic!

Setting the Stage

An erotic environment evokes all of the senses. You may start with a circle of dried or fresh rose petals or other flower petals. Create a large

enough circle for you and your beloved to be able to stretch out in, with room enough for food, drinks, massage oil, pillows, toys, and scents. Colorful fabrics or scarves may be draped over furniture to change the atmosphere. Set aside a special time for this celebration of the sensual, with no distractions such as phones, pets, computers, or televisions. Arrange for the kids to spend time at grandma's, or at a cousin's or friend's home. You owe yourselves this special time alone and it can nourish and

strengthen your relationship. Remember: You must first nourish yourself in order to nourish others.

Lighting

Intimate lighting can change the whole atmosphere of the evening. You can place candles

French sepia postcard, late nineteenth century.

around the room or outline the rim of your circle of flowers with votive candles set in small jars. Tiny holiday lights work well and provide subtle lighting. A colored scarf placed over a lamp or tacked around a ceiling light fixture can change the scenery, but watch that it does not burn. Soft lighting using a small lamp with a colored bulb can evoke dreamy and seductive qualities.

Temperature

Keeping the room warm can inspire thoughts of wearing less clothing. It is a good idea to stack some extra wood indoors for a fire before starting the evening's festivities. I remember one passionate but cold winter evening when the fire was getting low but the wood was outside. Wearing only my sheepskin boots and a fluffy

If one desires another's love, one must take an orange and prick it all over with a needle, then sleep with it under one's armpit. If the loved one then eats the orange, he or she will return love.

European folklore

red feather tied in my hair, I ran outside to fetch a log or two. I was standing bare-booty with my head in the woodshed when I noticed the neighbors' car pulling into our shared driveway—with its headlights on, of course. Caught with only two logs on, I waved!

The Bedroom

A trail of flowers leads toward and encircles the bed. How can you make the bedroom a rich erotic environment? What are some of the ways you could prepare this room to receive your most special lover? The bed could be dressed for the occasion in a set of new, colorful, slinky silk or fuzzy flannel sheets. Strings of small white or amber holiday lights hung over the bed give a warm glow to the room. Draping a few lengths of sheer fabric over the bed can give a cozy canopy effect, especially if you include some soft, fluffy, colorful pillows. Erotic art may be displayed to inspire and moisten thoughts and ideas. Scent the room by spritzing a seductive, fragrant mist and watch what unfolds. The bedding, pillows, and curtains can be sprayed with your personal fragrance to entice and lure. Have a playful picnic on your bed! Remember the massage oil or lotion and be sure to pick out fresh flowers to adorn the room, as they are sacred offerings to the goddesses of love.

Foods

Prepare a beautifully arranged tray of fruit and finger foods with bubbly beverages such as champagne or fruit sodas ahead of time for the evening, so you don't need to keep jumping up to get things. Snacking can be revitalizing during a passionate evening. If you enjoy cannabis, have a pipe or joints rolled and ready with a lighter and ashtray. Don't forget drinking water. You may wish to bring out your beautiful stemware, enchanting goblets, and special china.

Accessories

Have a special, sensual, silky robe just for these occasions. Shades of red, rose, and deep burgundy symbolize passion. Try black or red

Lord Frederic Leighton, *The Bath of Psyche,* 1890. Oil on canvas. Tate Gallery, London.

lingerie, if you usually wear white, and remember the magic of jewelry. Wear your hair differently or wrapped with twisted fabric; put on a touch of makeup to accentuate eyes and lips. By artfully adorning yourself, you are celebrating your beauty and honoring the god or goddess within.

Women and men have worn makeup since ancient times to be more sensually alluring. They often outlined their eyes with kohl to accentuate them and to protect against the evil eye. Women added color to their lips, cheeks, and eyes to make their faces appear as they do during sexual arousal. Henna, a plant-based coloring used to color the hair red, was also worn on the hands, feet, belly, and nipples as visually erotic artwork and for protection and blessing.

Let your inner wild woman or wild man inspire you to dress according to your mood or the phase of the moon. You may feel like wearing a loincloth and carrying a feather in your teeth for teasing, or dressing in a red silk robe, heels, and seductive lingerie. You may wish to start a collection of erotic clothing and adult toys. (It's probably best to leave the flannel teddy-bear jammies for another time!) Try silks, rayons, or velvets. Have you ever worn nothing but a silk scarf tied around you?

Soft, gentle music for relaxing or faster music with some good drumming for dancing can be collected ahead of time.

A Sequence of Events

You can start the day with a little note written about the evening's events. Why not begin by bathing together? Light candles, play soothing, sensuous music, or even take an aromatic and uplifting shower by sprinkling a few drops of essential oils onto the shower floor before stepping in. You may prefer your bath alone, or it may be shared with someone special. If you choose to share your bath, add liquid soap to a sea sponge to lather each other up. The tub awaits with aromatic bubbles, bath oil, or bath salts (see recipes). A sensuous bath is also a wonderful way to soothe PMS and helps anytime you need a little attitude adjustment. Try putting in a handful or two of dried seaweed, which has a scent reminiscent of the sea, good for channeling your siren or mermaid self. Greens, blues, and all oceanic colors help set the mood. A couple of drops of food coloring makes the

bath a beautiful blue-green without dyeing your skin. (Yellow, however, is not a bathwater color conducive to passion!)

Don't soak too long, as it can be overly relaxing. You may need to finish off with a cold spray to revive you from too hot a bath! A trail of flower petals now invites you to an arrangement of flowers, fruits, and shells in honor of Aphrodite. Candlelight flickers. Beautiful goblets await, filled with a magical love elixir (see recipes). Toast each other:

May your cup be filled with the
sweetest nectar of love.

Sensual spray mists (see recipes) to scent the air and refresh the body may be used.

Anointing the body with fragrant oils or amber may be done now. Oil of rose, sandalwood, patchouli, jasmine, ylang ylang, or your favorite scent can be used. With a drop on your finger anoint the top of the head, with blessings to invoke the most sacred self to open to its beauty within. Anoint the heart center, that the person may open her heart, or his, to sensuality. The breasts and genitals may be blessed with oil, honoring their strength and their gifts of life and pleasure. With hands upon each other's hearts, looking into each other's eyes, speak what is in your hearts. The god or goddess of love may be invoked to inspire and renew.

Whether the celebration includes self- or mutual pleasuring, remember that you can dedicate that beautiful, sacred pleasure and orgasm to whatever you want to bring into your life. Dedicate them to radiant health, a new, more appropriate job, a reliable car, a more comfortable home, or a special healing for you or others. Dedicating orgasms and sexual joy helps to return some of that beautiful energy to nurture our Earth Mother. Making love heals and nourishes our bodies, which heals and feeds our planet.

A wonderful thing to do for someone is to

or both of the bowls and slowly feed each other, using your fingers. Or place a grape on your tongue and have your lover try to kiss it from you or offer it as a fruit kiss. In between bites, you might share an enchanting rose punch or May wine. . . . *Oops, some chocolate dripped upon your breast. This will need to be licked off . . .*

A wonderful exercise is to take one grape or one slice of orange or other piece of fruit or bread and very, very slowly, cell by cell, eat and nibble at the fruit, experiencing every sensation, flavor, and texture. Take several minutes to do this.

Serve yourself as dessert. . . . You may wish to place a tablecloth down first. Lie down, then decorate your naked breasts or whole body with pieces of cake with strawberries, whipped cream, chocolate chips, and any of your favorite frozen yogurt sprinkles or your favorite dessert. (Maybe *not* cherries jubilee!) You are now ready to serve!

cover his naked body with a large veil of silk. Have him lie down first. Then very, very slowly pull one end so that it slides off tantalizingly slowly until the very last corner is lifted away.

The Sensuous Fruit Feast

A silver tray of seductively stuffed dates scented with rose water, and a large platter of bite-sized pieces of fruits such as oranges, apples, bananas, kiwis, berries, pears, grapes, pineapple, mango, and papaya await dipping. Have one bowl of whipped cream and one bowl of chocolate sauce ready. Begin by dipping a piece of fruit in one

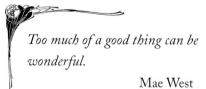

Too much of a good thing can be wonderful.

Mae West

Chapter 3

Aphrodisiacs

Aphrodisiacs can be different things to different people. Aphrodisiacs can be stimulating, relaxing, and nourishing. One person may need to feel more relaxed to be able to feel more sensual. Another person may need to be stimulated to feel more aroused. For yet another person the best aphrodisiac can be starting the day with a good, nourishing breakfast.

The milk of a white cow who has a white calf nestling beside her possesses excellent aphrodisiac properties and if drunk, lengthens one's life and brings fame and fortune.

Vatsyayana, *Kama Sutra,*
fourth-century Hindu love manual

One time at the herbal apothecary shop where I worked, a very tense, stressed-out, and agitated man appeared, practically begging me for "something, you know—I have a hot date tonight!" The poor guy needed something relaxing very soon or he would either collapse or explode right there and then. So I gave him valerian root (as a favorite herbal teacher of mine had once suggested), which is a relaxant. I figured he couldn't do anything with his date unless he relaxed a bit. He came back a couple of days later, beaming, to tell me that the root I gave him had had a powerful aphrodisiac effect that evening! He wanted more, even though it smelled a little strange. For him, as for many of us, all that was needed was to relax into his sensual self to have a great time. Many people have different experiences with valerian. It can be strongly relaxing for some, while keeping a small percentage of people awake.

Many mothers come to me, tired and stressed from all their mothering activities. Typically, they have finished the day's chores and simply want to lie down, weary to the bone. For them, something more stimulating could be helpful, like inhaling essential oil of rosemary or basil, or peppermint with lemon oil. Chocolate, cayenne, ginger, yerba maté tea, or a stimulating bath with fragrances can also pep up a special evening.

If you feel depleted, exhausted, or stressed, and are not feeling responsive or interested, regular, nourishing herbal tonics and rest can restore proper functioning of the body and increase vitality, as well as help you to feel juicy when you want to be. It is more difficult to experience pleasure when the body is out of balance and run-down. Three balanced meals each day has worked wonders for many busy folks. Starting the day with a good breakfast or brunch will help those who feel an energy depletion in the late afternoon. For dinner, try to include at least three different colors of food: greens, golden yellows, rich oranges and reds, blues, beiges, and browns. This will ensure that you get a range of vitamins and minerals in your diet.

If the body is full of vitality,
is at ease,
and the mind is poised
and at peace,
sex can be a powerful expression
of that vitality.

David Hoffmann,
The Complete Illustrated Holistic Herbal

An Arousing Array of Libido-Lifting Favorites: Stimulating Aphrodisiacs

Aromatic Seeds

Aromatic seeds carry the potential of new life within. Caraway, dill, fennel, anise, cumin, coriander, and cardamom are not only tasty digestive aids when chewed, but they can enhance the effects of estrogen in the body. Fennel seed given to new mothers produces abundant milk and is a favorite in the Mediterranean. These seeds can be chewed or ground and mixed with honey or tea and used to flavor liqueurs and cordials. They also sweeten the breath!

Aromatic seeds traditionally have been boiled in milk with spices, like chai tea. In the *Kama Sutra*, a classical East Indian treatise on the art of making love, there is mention of a preparation said to increase sexual vigor. It combines equal parts ghee (clarified butter), honey, fennel seeds, and milk. (I wonder, would this be applied to the body or spread on pancakes, or both?)

Cardamom (Elettaria cardamomum)

A favored spice in both Indian and Arab kitchens, cardamom has aphrodisiac properties and is also used as a breath sweetener. Add to rice pudding with rose water and chopped dates or sprinkle on a fruit salad with toasted nuts and seeds. A wonderful seedy recipe is to grind $1/3$ cup each white sesame seeds and flaxseed, then add 1 tablespoon cardamom and 2 tablespoons Sucanat (unrefined sugar). This can be eaten on cereal or with yogurt and is tasty plain. It provides Omega III oils, calcium, and protein. Thanks to herbalist Mindy Green for this favorite recipe.

Chocolate (Theobroma cacao)

A luscious aphrodisiac and stimulant, chocolate raises our endorphins. The word *chocolate* is said to derive from the Mayan *xocolatl* (pronounced "shocolatl"). Aztec legend held that cacao seeds had been brought from paradise and

Brain Food

The body's central organ of sexual response is the brain!

Stimulate and nourish your brain with magic scents, luscious tastes, favorite colors, warm baths, fragrant flowers, candlelight, the feel of silk against your naked body, chocolate, wine, liqueurs, written and visual erotica, sensual massage, feathers, skinny-dipping, and moonlight.

Brain Tonic

Ginkgo leaves—4 parts
Gota kola leaves—2 parts
Rosemary leaves—1 part
Yerba maté leaves—2 parts
Peppermint leaves—1 part
Cinnamon sticks—1 part

Combine the dried herbs and store in an airtight container.

For tea: Use 2 teaspoons for each cup of boiling water and steep 10 minutes. Strain and sweeten if desired. For a wine cordial: Steep 1½ cups of the blend in 1 liter of wine for 1 week. Strain and sweeten. For a tincture or liqueur: In a jar, cover the dried herbs completely with brandy or vodka for 2–3 weeks, strain for tincture, using 1 teaspoon 2–3 times daily. For a liqueur, sweeten the tincture with honey, sugar, or maple syrup, using ½–1 cup for each liter of alcohol.

that wisdom and power came from eating the fruit of the cacao tree. Chili powder, cinnamon, cloves, anise, and vanilla are added to the cocoa drink. The seeds are cocoa-brown and look like dried lima beans. They are very bitter and sugar is added to give us our favorite familiar sweet.

Chocolate was first noted in 1519 when the Spanish explorer Cortez visited the court of Emperor Montezuma of Mexico. It was said that Montezuma took no other beverage than the chocolatl, a potion of chocolate flavored with vanilla, cayenne, and cinnamon. This beverage was prepared by being reduced to a froth the consistency of honey, which was taken cold and would gradually dissolve in the mouth. Montezuma would consume this in goblets before entering his harem.

Women often crave chocolate as their hormones shift, perhaps for that sense of well-being or feeling of being in love it can provide. Chocolate is rich in magnesium and copper and is wonderful for raising the spirit. Try not to chew it; let it slowly melt in your mouth and savor the taste. It melts at body temperature, so allow your imagination free reign.

During a visit to Belize, as the warm morning breeze brought me the intoxicating scent of white ginger blossoms, Dr. Rosita Arvigo kindly made me chocolate tea! In a cup she placed 1 heaping spoonful of quality pinkish-brown chocolate powder, 1 spoon of light brown sugar, a pinch of cinnamon, and a spoon of vanilla extract. She added hot water and stirred well as a spiced vanilla–dark chocolate aroma wafted past me. When I recreate this at home, I close my eyes, inhale the richness, and am back in Belize.

Did you know the word "stressed" spelled backward is "desserts"? Oh, O!

Damiana (Turnera diffusa)

Damiana was once known as *Turnera aphrodisiaca,* suggesting it was used as an aphrodisiac. Its fragrant leaves come to us from Central America and are related to the mint family. Ancient Aztecs used the leaves as a most powerful sexual tonic and stimulant, second only to chocolate. What I like to do with them is to make tea and liqueur. In Mexico even the children drink it as a tonic and refreshing beverage. (I don't think I would give it to a teenager.) It is also used as a nerve tonic and is slightly warming and stimulating, but not like caffeine. It makes an excellent iced tea when mixed with spearmint and rose petals. Some folks enjoy smoking 2 pinches of damiana with a pinch of spearmint or peppermint leaves, a pinch of passionflower, and a few rose petals torn into pieces. It is also an antidepressant and urinary antiseptic. As a cordial, use for flavoring (see Libidinous Libations).

In ancient times this cordial was made by the Guayacura tribe from the damiana growing wild in the Baja desert. They drank it in centuries-old ceremonies, but according to legend it had such incredible aphrodisiac powers that the Guayacura chief banned its consumption. Today its use is confined to mothers-in-law, who give it as a gift in hopes of becoming grandmothers.

When you make the damiana cordial yourself, the trick is to remember to let it sit long enough—the longer it sits, the better its flavor. It can be quite potent so a little will go a long way. Cordials are meant to be sipped, diluted, or used as a flavoring. They are good diluted with carbonated water. A quick way to make a damiana cordial is to take 1 cup of commercially prepared vanilla extract and add 2 tablespoons of damiana leaves and 1 tablespoon of honey, sugar, or maple syrup. Stir well and let the mixture sit for a week before straining through cheesecloth.

Muira Puama
(Ptychopetalum olacoides)

Muira puama, also known as "potency wood" or "tree of virility," comes from the Brazilian Amazon. It is used as a tonic to treat neuromuscular problems. Taken as tea it is used to treat sexual debility and is claimed to prevent baldness as well. An aphrodisiac, it is also a stimulant. Native people traditionally chewed the bark or cooked it up as a tea. It can also be smoked or prepared by gently simmering 4 tablespoons of bark in 1 cup of brandy for 15 minutes. Strain it and sip one or two very small cordial glasses. (One cordial glass is approximately 2–3 teaspoons.)

Prickly Ash Bark
(Zanthoxylum americanum)

Traditionally used to increase circulation, especially to the lower part of the body, prickly ash bark is useful if you sit a lot during the day. Simmer 1–2 teaspoons of the bark in 1 cup of water for 5–7 minutes. Strain and drink 1 cup. Try a little cinnamon to flavor the tea.

Rosemary (Rosmarinus officinalis)

Rosemary aids circulation throughout the body, and its taste is refreshing and uplifting. Since rosemary symbolizes remembrance, it is used in weddings, and an old custom of sprinkling the bridal bed with it to ensure conjugal bliss still persists in some parts of Europe. Steep a handful of fresh rosemary in a pitcher of lemonade in the refrigerator for a couple hours. If using frozen lemonade concentrate, instead of adding the recommended 4 cans of water, try adding 4 cans of cooled rosemary tea to the lemonade concentrate.

Saffron (Crocus sativus)

Saffron was used by the ancient Phoenicians as a love spice to flavor the moon-shaped cakes eaten in honor of Ashtoreth, the goddess of fertility. Saffron is also a bridal spice and is used as a beautiful golden-yellow dye for foods. Take

a few threads of saffron and steep them in a spoonful of boiling water. Let it sit a few minutes, then use the colored water in rice, pasta, or potato salad.

Sweet Basil (Ocimum basilicum)

In Italy basil symbolizes love. This is not only great on pasta, rice, potatoes, veggies, and pizza—why not try an edible pesto massage oil? Blend together 1 cup of oil with 2 teaspoons of pesto. Great as an appetizer—pesto thighs!

I think one of my earliest fragrant memories is of being in my Nana's little garden while she picked fresh basil. She would tuck a sprig of it in her cleavage so its scent would be released throughout the day. She often gave me big hugs and, as I was not that tall then, my nose would smush right there into the basil. Ah, Nana's magical basil hugs!

Vanilla (Vanilla planifolia)

A favorite of mine, vanilla has a delectable, luscious scent and flavor. I have included it with the stimulating herbs because its fragrance is stimulating to the senses. Vanilla is actually the

Flirting!

A great aphrodisiac, not to be forgotten, is *flirting!* Flirting stimulates estrogen production, which can arouse women's libidos. Our culture has forgotten the dance of life, that ritual invitation to love so well demonstrated in nature. Where is that lusty, juice-provoking, teasing, flirting, playful dance? One spring evening I was watching two beautiful mockingbirds on a fence and was captivated and inspired by their mating dance. As he approached her, she scooted away; he looked away, then she neared him a little; he moved in closer, and she flew up and over him and landed on the other side! As though to say, "Yes! Yes! Oh, but not so close yet! Well, maybe now, but not too close, oh, yes! Yes!"

ripened seed pod from a tropical orchid and is one of the ingredients in good chocolate. It is a scent as much as a taste, and many people are reminded of pleasant memories when they smell it. Vanilla has long been a favorite of mine—I remember wearing the extract as cologne in high school!

One rainy day I had to keep my son and a few of his friends busy. I decided to put one drop each of different essential oils on cotton balls and pass them around to see if the children could guess what was what. I used orange, anise, lemon, spearmint, peppermint, almond, and vanilla. Each of the children guessed vanilla to be chocolate! When I told them it was vanilla, they could hardly believe me. Vanilla is used in making chocolate bars, and that was the scent they associated with when eating chocolate.

To use vanilla pods, choose ones that are slightly soft, not dried up and hard. Slice the pod lengthwise and scrape out the gazillions of seeds to flavor fruit, baked goods, honey, sugar, egg dishes, granola, or a cinnamon–vanilla sauce. Use the extract on sliced peaches or strawberries, fruit salads, and beverages. Add it to liqueurs and teas, or put it in the bath! You can easily make your own vanilla extract by slicing the pod lengthwise, then chopping 2 vanilla beans for each ounce of brandy, and steeping for 1 month. To make vanilla tea combine in a mug 2 teaspoons of vanilla extract, 1 teaspoon of raw sugar, honey, or maple syrup, and add boiling water. Let sit a minute or so. Sip and enjoy! Try adding vanilla extract to your favorite wine, tea, or juice.

Yerba Maté (Ilex paraguayensis)

A pleasant, slightly smoky tea, yerba maté is warming and stimulating. Since it has much less caffeine than coffee, it is great for those who do not wish to or cannot drink coffee yet desire to remain awake or revived and more alert. Yerba maté is traditionally shared in a gourd bowl with a silver straw in South America. Steep 1 teaspoon of the leaves in 1 cup hot water for 7–10 minutes.

Sir Lawrence Alma-Tadema, *Ask Me No More*, 1906. Oil on canvas. Private collection.

Yohimbé (Corynanthe yohimbe)

This plant is traditionally used by the West African Bantu tribes as a sacrament for matrimony. Its active constituent reacts with the hydrochloric acid in digestive juices to become assimilated by the body. It is a central nervous system stimulant and can be harmful if used by anyone who has high blood pressure. Weak limbs, a vague restlessness, chills and shivers with dizziness and nausea may be experienced

In Praise of Vanilla

Craving vanilla, I start the bathwater gushing, and unscrew the lid of a heavy glass jar of Ann Steeger of Paris's Bain Crème, *senteur vanille.* A wallop of potent vanilla hits my nose as I reach into the lotion, let it seep through my fingers, and carry a handful to the faucet. Fragrant bubbles fill the tub. A large bar of vanilla bath soap, sitting in an antique porcelain dish, acts as an aromatic beacon. While I steep in waves of vanilla, a friend brings me a vanilla cream seltzer, followed by a custard made with vanilla beans that have come all the way from Madagascar. Brown flecks float through the creamy yellow curds. . . .

When I finally emerge from the tub, . . . I apply Ann Steeger's vanilla body veil, which smells edible and thick as smoke. Then Jean Laporte's Vanilla perfume, vanilla with a bitter sting. The inside of a vanilla bean contains a figlike marrow, and if I were to scrape some out, I could prepare spicy vanilla bisque for dinner, followed by chicken in a vanilla glaze, salad with vanilla vinaigrette, vanilla ice cream with a sauce of chestnuts in vanilla marinade, followed by warm brandy flavored with chopped vanilla pod, and then, in a divine vanilla stupor, seep into bed and fall into a heavy orchidlike sleep!

Diane Ackerman,
A Natural History of the Senses

as side effects. (Really romantic!) There are some fairly good products on the market that use this plant in combination with other plants. *Please use with caution!* In my experience, it left me edgy, nervous, quite irritable, and unable to sleep even hours later.

Warming and Stimulating Herbs

Cinnamon and ginger, along with cayenne and curry, are excellent for increasing our circulation and getting those cold feet warmed up! These spices can be added to our food, used as teas, or steeped in brandy. Cinnamon and ginger can be added to honeys, nut butters, fruit salads, and breads.

Cinnamon (Cinnamomum cassia)

This well-known kitchen spice has also been used through the centuries as an aphrodisiac and is one of the most popular tastes as well as scents. In a recent survey, cinnamon's warm, spicy, woody fragrance baking in an oven was judged as the most sensually stimulating aroma, so enjoying a warm cinnamon roll may help to start your day on the juicy side. A spicy tea made with a handful of cinnamon sticks to a teapot of water or apple cider is not only warming but can also be erotically stimulating. Cinnamon with ginger, cardamom, and cloves is an "olde thyme" favorite in cakes, muffins, cookies, and breads. Imagine pumpkin pies as aphrodisiacs. That could be something to be thankful for.

Ginger (Zingiber officinale)

From Asia to Turkey, India to the Arabian desert, ginger has a strong reputation as a powerful aphrodisiac. In the book *The Perfumed Garden* it is recommended that ginger be used externally as well as internally. Ginger ointments were used in stimulating massages for the abdomen. Ginger was also chewed with cubeb berries and spices, then the saliva was applied to the genitals. Hot and spicy! Try making your own ginger ale (see recipes). A couple of spoonfuls of powdered ginger may be added to a footbath, just the thing for "cold feet." You may find yourself hot and bothered!

To make ginger honey, peel and thinly slice about ½ cup of fresh ginger and place in a small jar. Gently warm about ½ cup of honey by placing the honey container in a pan of hot water until the honey is fluid. Pour this over the fresh ginger and with a chopstick release all of the air bubbles, making sure the ginger is covered. Let the ginger honey steep for about a week.

You will notice the honey becoming thinner as it extracts the water from the fresh ginger. The honey will taste gingery and the ginger may be eaten as candy. Keep refrigerated.

Nourishing Tonics As Aphrodisiacs

Burdock Root (Arctium lappa)

A nourishing tonic to the liver and blood, burdock makes a tasty tea or broth. Use fresh or dried root. The fresh root is delicious stir-fried. For the tea, gently simmer 1 large spoonful of roots in a cup of water for 10 minutes.

Ginkgo Leaves (Ginkgo biloba)

Ginkgo is used to bring more oxygen to the brain and aid circulation to the extremities. It is excellent for concentration and . . . what was the other thing? Oh, yes, I almost forgot. Memory! I steep the golden leaves (collected in the autumn) in my favorite blush wine for a week in the refrigerator. Sometimes I add mashed strawberries or raspberries.

Ginseng (Panax *spp.*) *and Siberian Ginseng* (Eleutherococcus senticosus)

Both the Chinese *Panax* and the Siberian ginsengs are restorative tonics. Siberian ginseng is the one I prefer to use as an adrenal tonic and as a help in adapting to stress. This ginseng *(Eleutherococcus senticosus)* is safe for people of all ages from kids to the elderly. A spoonful of Siberian ginseng powder can be taken mixed with honey. I would use the Chinese *Panax* ginseng for men who are run-down and who need to increase their vitality and life force. Small vials of the extract may be found in herb shops or natural food stores.

In *Herbs for Health and Healing* herbalist Kathi Keville recommends this nourishing blend for men "to help increase physical stamina and strengthen the adrenal glands so that they can take over producing sufficient hormones and tone the liver to help it properly detoxify": 1-ounce tincture of ginseng root, 1/2 ounce each tincture of Siberian ginseng root, Schizandra berries, and licorice root. Combine tinctures. Take 1/2 dropperful 1–2 times a day.

Licorice Root (Glycyrrhiza glabra)

Licorice root in small amounts can be a tonic to the adrenal glands, and due to its estrogen-enhancing effect in the body it helps promote juiciness. Remember to use this root in small amounts only. Add a pinch to the teapot as a sweetener or try a small spoonful of licorice root boiled in milk with a pinch each of black pepper, cinnamon, and ginger.

Nettle (Urtica dioica)

If I had to choose just one herb that best nourishes, tones, and strengthens the entire body—including the hair, skin, blood, bones, and glands—it would be nettle leaves. Dark green and one of the highest sources of plant iron as well as calcium, magnesium, and potassium, nettle plants provide nourishment to all. As a tea or, as I prefer, a brew, a handful of the leaves (about 1 cup) are steeped in 1 liter of boiled water overnight, then strained and drunk as a mineral-rich tonic for all the body systems. One or two cups daily bring the body "bio-available" minerals. Nettle can be found in the wild growing in moist, nitrogen-rich soil in areas with some shade. This plant draws the minerals from the soil into its leaves. We collect and make tea out of the leaves, steeping the tea long enough to extract the minerals into the water. Then we easily absorb the usable minerals into our system. The plant does all the work for us!

Nettle plants may also be steeped in wine, refrigerated, then sweetened if desired with maple syrup or other sweetener. Nettle leaves may be soaked in vinegar with garlic for a week, then added to veggies, rice, potatoes, or salad. Nettle may be a substitute for spinach in recipes such as lasagne, spanikopita, soups, and quiches.

For a rich nettle tonic, put on some gloves in the spring and collect enough nettle leaves to fill a gallon jar. Brush these off and rinse them, then cook them in a veggie or chicken broth until tender, 15–20 minutes. Puree the nettle leaves in a blender with $1/2$ cup of kefir or feta cheese. The nourishment provided by a cup of this tonic can be immediately felt—something really good you have done for yourself.

Oats (Avena sativa)

Do you remember the saying "Sow your wild oats"? It's a perfect example of the influence of nature and plants on our sexual lexicon.

Oats are a wild grass that may have originated in the Middle East and in the Mediterranean basin. Some of the earliest evidence of their use dates to 1000 B.C.E. and is found in cave dwellings in areas in Switzerland. Both cultivated and wild oats, possibly of Asian origin, were known to the ancient Greeks. Oats are known to have provided the Scots with hardiness, strength, and virility; they have been a major part of the Scots' diet for over two thousand years. The use of oats by early Germanic and eastern European tribes may have provided the strength used to take down the Roman Empire. This food has been eaten throughout the ages to strengthen the entire body and to increase vigor and vitality. Are you "feeling your oats"? They are nourishing to the nervous system, are considered an excellent nerve tonic, and have an antidepressant effect. In the form of oatstraw tea, they are very mineral-rich. The oat straw is the whole plant that our oatmeal comes from and is best picked in the spring in its green, milky stage. Eating oatmeal is very nourishing, comforting, and tonifying. Could oatmeal-spice cookies be aphrodisiac? I believe so, especially if vanilla and chocolate chips are added.

Rose (Rosa sp.)

Over time one of the favorite stimuli to love and passion has been and still is the rose. Giving a woman a dozen longstem red roses is an instantaneous aphrodisiac and the ultimate acknowledgment of her desirable passion. When we take in the beauty of the rose we are reminded of women's beautiful soft nether petals. Flowers are the genitals of the plant and they beckon us to approach and delight in their fragrance and beauty. Roses have long been given as gifts to beautiful women. Among aromatherapists it is thought that Cleopatra welcomed Marc Antony into her chamber with rose petals more than a foot deep covering her floor. She also soaked the sails of her ship in rose water to perfume the breezes.

Our Victorian sisters used to pick petals from the most fragrant old varieties of roses and cover them with egg whites beaten with a little water. Then they dusted them in superfine sugar to crystallize them and dried the petals on parchment in an oven set at a very low temperature with the door open for a few minutes. Mint leaves, lemon balm leaves, violets, and heartsease may also be crystallized this way. They make beautiful cake decorations.

One of my favorite things to do is to collect dried rose petals in a special container and sprinkle them around on romantic evenings to create a sacred space. Later I gather them up and use them again. If you do this, keep them out of sunlight, as they fade easily. If you can find the old varieties, use them, as they are the most fragrant.

Rose water can be sprayed on the body or added to a bath or beverage. Make sure the rose water you buy is distilled, so that you get the true essence of the rose and not a cheap synthetic.

A delicate rose syrup is made by stirring $1/4$ cup of rose water into 1 cup of light honey. This may be added to tea or carbonated mineral water or drizzled over fruit or nipples.

Sarsaparilla (Smilax sp.)

This root can aid testosterone production in the body and is a glandular and prostate tonic for men. It is used as a tea, tincture, or liqueur. For tea, gently simmer 2 teaspoons in 1 cup water for 7–10 minutes. Strain, sweeten with honey or maple syrup. The roots steeped in brandy with honey and spices make a wonderful elixir.

Saw Palmetto Berries (Serenoa repens)

These pungent reddish berries from the saw palmetto palm tree have long been used as a

day. Take $^1/_2$–1 teaspoon of the tincture 2–3 times a day.

Turmeric (Curcuma longa)

Primarily used in the preparation of curry, giving it the rich, golden yellow color, tumeric is highly prized in India as a love stimulant. It was also used as a vaginal douche! Turmeric is taken as a tonic for the liver. A sprinkle added to rice, potatoes, eggs, or veggie dishes brightens up the plate.

Vitex agnus-castus *Berries,* or *Chaste Tree Berries*

Vitex is a plant that comes to us from the Mediterranean. Historically used as an *an*aphrodisiac to reduce amorous intent in monks, *Vitex agnus-castus* is also known as "monk's pepper tree." These berries are used to balance female hormones, tone the uterus, and nourish the reproductive system. *Vitex* needs to be taken for a minimum of two months. Some women no-

safe and efficient tonic for the male reproductive system. These berries are very nourishing and antibacterial. Saw palmetto may be taken as a preventive tonic to help avoid prostate problems and it is very helpful once there is infection. Traditionally it is mixed with equal parts of damiana. Take two '00' capsules 3 times a

The Rose Gatherers, Rudolph Ernst, 1854–1920.

tice results quickly, while others may take longer. From pubescent acne and menstrual cramping to menopausal imbalances—*Vitex* can help to normalize the system. Many women claim it has helped their libido, while others say it reduces it temporarily until their bodies are back in balance. I would recommend this tonic if you have many symptoms of imbalance in the reproductive system.

Hormonal Herbs

Nourishing our hormonal system is very important to keep us healthy, vital, sensuous, and interested. When the time comes for the ovaries to cease estrogen production, the adrenal glands take over—but only if they are healthy and not exhausted. Siberian ginseng is a specific adrenal stress tonic. Try this elixir: Mix 3 parts Siberian ginseng root and 1 part cinnamon pieces with ¹/₂ part licorice root. This makes tasty tea; it is also good steeped and covered in brandy for 2 weeks.

Many plants provide nourishment to the hormonal system. The berries of the *Vitex agnus-castus* shrub used as a tea or extract can help normalize women's hormones. The scent of rose geranium is also very balancing for women and their hormones, having an uplifting yet soothing effect.

Women's Balancing Blend

This needs to be taken for at least two months or two moons to help normalize the hormones, especially if you are experiencing symptoms of imbalance. The liver is nourished and supported by this blend.

> *Vitex* berries—3 parts (crush berries slightly with a mortar and pestle or in a coffee or spice grinder)
> Burdock root—2 parts
> Licorice root —¹/₂ part (optional if you do not care for the taste of licorice)

Combine dried ingredients and keep the blend in a jar out of bright light. To make tea, take a heaping teaspoonful of blend for each cup of tea and add it to 1 cup of water. Bring this to a gentle simmer, and heat over a very low flame with the lid on for 10 minutes. Strain the herbs and sip the tea hot or warm. Start with 1 cup a day, then work up to 3 cups a day if there are many or intense symptoms of hormonal imbalance. Some women find that 1 cup a day is just what they need to feel balanced. Others may need to make a pot of tea and drink it throughout the day and evening.

Men's Tonic, A Great "Boner Toner"

These herbs act as tonics and supports for the liver, prostate, circulatory system, adrenals, and nerves.

> Sarsaparilla root—2 parts
> Saw palmetto berries—1 part
> Ginger root—2 parts
> Cinnamon chips—1 part

Prickly ash bark—1 part
Burdock root—1 part
Green oats—2 parts
Licorice root—1 part
Siberian ginseng root—1 part (or substitute Chinese root)
Ginkgo leaf—3 parts
Vanilla extract or orange peel, optional

For a tea this may be simmered in apple cider or water. For a tincture use brandy as a base. This may be sweet enough with the licorice root in it, or maple syrup or honey may be added to taste. A spoonful or two of vanilla extract or orange peel may be added for flavor and enjoyment.

Minerals and Vitamins

There are a number of nutrient components that should be included in our daily diet, as they are fundamental to a healthy libido as well as to general health. Among the minerals and vitamins involved, the following are crucial:

- **Zinc**—Vital for proper functioning of the reproductive systems for both women and men, zinc is found in oysters, abalone, and sea veggies such as dulse and kelp, as well as in spirulina and chickweed. Supplements of 50–100 milligrams daily may be taken with a meal. A handful of pumpkin seeds provides a rich source of zinc, as well as vitamins E and F.

- **Iron**—The need for iron is higher in women, since we need to replace iron that is lost through our menstrual cycles. We can do this with herbs, foods, or supplements. One of the first things to go if you tend toward being anemic is the sex drive. This can be remedied with iron-rich herbs and foods: nettles, yellow dock root, dark leafy greens, chickweed, kelp, burdock, and dandelion root; molasses and dried fruits; figs, raisins, cherries, apricots, and prunes and their juice; bittersweet chocolate; and whole grains.
- **Iodine**—This mineral is important for a properly functioning thyroid gland. If thyroid activity is sluggish, the libido can be slowed to a halt. Iodine is found in sea veggies such as dulse, kelp, and nori. Iodine supplements are also available.

Vitamin supplements have been found to boost vitality and stamina. Don't forget a good B-complex with C for stress. Vitamins E and F are the "sexy" vitamins and are found in many seeds, including sesame, sunflower, and pumpkin seeds.

- **Vitamin E** is found in leafy greens and seeds. Start by working up from 400 to 1,000 international units a day taken with a meal. It can really juice you up, as well as help prevent breast problems, vaginal dryness, and menopausal discomforts. Vitamin E is important for both women and men.
- **Vitamin F** is found in essential fatty acids, the good oils that are so important to our glands, skin, hair, and hormone production. Cleopatra was known to eat sesame every day, which may have contributed to her reputation as an exquisite seductress. Vitamin F is also found in olive oil, sesame oil, hemp seed oil, and the oils of evening primrose, black

currant, borage, flaxseed, and purslane leaves.

Mineral-Rich Brew

An excellent, nourishing, tonic tea can be easily made by combining equal parts of the following herbs. Use 1 handful of the blend for a large pot of tea. Let the tea steep for longer than the usual 10 minutes. It may steep overnight in the refrigerator or for at least 1 to 4 hours. This way much more of the herbs can be extracted into the water. Spearmint or peppermint leaves may be added to the brew.

> Nettle leaves
> Green oats
> Red raspberry leaf
> Red clover blossoms
> Lemongrass

Bitters Digestive Tonic

Suffering from too many pleasures? For that morning after a wild weekend, be kind to your liver with a liver "detox" tea when you have overdone the chocolate sauce, cordials, and garlic honey. Bitters provide a detoxifying action.

Bitters are taken before meals to stimulate the digestive juices, to encourage the appetite, to help prevent gas, bloating, and indigestion after meals, and to lift the spirits. If you had a wild night of drinking and eating some interesting food combinations, it is helpful to drink a hot cup of this tea before retiring and again the morning after to dispel hangovers.

> Gentian root—2 parts
> Orange peel—$^1/_2$ part
> Aniseed—$^1/_2$ part
> Ginger—$^1/_2$ part

Blend the herbs and use 1 spoonful for each cup of boiling water for tea. This combination is also excellent in port wine, sweetened with a spoonful of honey.

Or maybe you have a touch of "honeymooner's annoyance," otherwise known as cystitis or bladder irritation? An excellent remedy to soothe the irritated tissues is equal parts of:

> Uva ursi leaves
> Corn silk
> Cleavers
> Dandelion leaf
> Lemongrass

Make a hot tea of this combination to drink 2–3 times a day and add extra, green leafy foods to your diet, including parsley and cilantro. Cranberry juice is helpful, and a shot or two of carrot juice will increase your vitamin A intake and help boost your immune system.

Honey

An ancient food found perfectly preserved in King Tut's tomb, honey has been used in many cultures, primarily as an aphrodisiac. Electuaries were taken as a pleasant way to ingest healing herbs. An electuary is a powdered herb mixed with honey. You can stir different aromatic herbs and spices into honey, which can then be added to hot tea, toast, or toes! Flavored honeys may be delectably drizzled on certain erogenous zones and then licked off! An ancient aphrodisiac was powdered aniseed mixed with honey and applied to the genitals. This was believed to increase fertility and virility. Be careful if you are outdoors— you may attract bees. (In France it is thought that if you are stung by a bee you have been inoculated with a potent aphrodisiac. But for the Hindus it is the bee's honey that is nature's elixir and love's nectar.)

Grind unsprayed fragrant roses to a powder in a coffee or spice grinder and mix into honey for a beautiful pink color. Try using fresh lavender flowers, ground anise or fennel seeds, ground cardamom, or a pinch of cayenne powder. Chocolate and peppermint or orange peel with aniseed are my favorites. Cocoa powder stirred into honey with a drop of peppermint oil added or orange zest with ground aniseeds added make a sensuous combination. Make vanilla-spiced honey by mixing a spoonful of vanilla extract into 4 ounces of honey, stirring well. For an exotically lustful honey, cover 1 head of pressed fresh garlic with enough honey to completely cover the garlic. Shake the jar each day for 3–4 weeks; you will notice the honey becoming more liquidy. This garlic honey is wonderful spread on toasted French bread or a lover's toes. Pumpkin pie spices added to and left in the honey along with a dash of vanilla extract yield a deep chocolate-brown, heavenly, spiced honey. Make your own baking-spice blend by stirring together $1\frac{1}{2}$ tablespoons of ground cinnamon, $\frac{1}{2}$ teaspoon of ground ginger, and $\frac{1}{4}$ teaspoon each of allspice powder, ground cloves, and nutmeg.

Edible Body Paints

Try mixing some of your favorite fruit jams with honey to create raspberry-, boysenberry-, apricot-, strawberry-, or plum-honey sauces. These are fun to paint the body with for dessert and they easily wash off in the shower. Honey is a humectant, which means it draws moisture to the skin. It could easily draw lips, tongue, and other body parts to the skin as well!

Fresh chopped mint leaves or sliced fresh ginger may be stirred well into the honey with a chopstick to make sure all the air bubbles are out. You may notice the honey becoming more liquidy as it extracts the water from the fresh plant. Leave at room temperature for a week, then strain through cheesecloth. If the honey thickens or crystallizes, place the jar in a pan of hot water and simmer gently until the honey is clear.

For an instant flavored honey, add 1–2 drops of essential oil to about $\frac{1}{4}$ cup of honey. Stir well with a chopstick. Rose essential oil, orange blossom oil, rose geranium oil, mint, anise, lemon, and orange oils are delicious and make nice gifts also.

Relaxing Aphrodisiacs

Ashwaganda (Withania somnifera)

A nourishing and relaxing adrenal tonic, ashwaganda is used to enhance the libido. A traditional East Indian recipe calls for 2–4 grams of the powdered root to be simmered in milk with a little ginger, honey to taste, and a pinch of cinnamon. This is excellent for debility and exhaustion.

Cannabis (Cannabis sativa)

Cannabis can be a stimulating aphrodisiac at first, then a sedative. Traditionally smoked or eaten in delicacies and sweets, cannabis has been used since antiquity as a sensuality-enhancing aphrodisiac. One of the oldest archaeological relics in existence is a fragment of hemp cloth found at Catal Huyuk that dates to about 8000 B.C.E. The plant is mentioned as an aphrodisiac in Assyrian texts, where it is called *qu-nu-bu*. In Istanbul pastilles were made from hashish, honey, saffron, ginger, fennel seeds, cardamom, and roses. Hemp seeds were customarily roasted and salted and served at wedding dinners. During medieval times, cannabis was taken as a ritual drink or ceremonial sherbet in the temples of India to reach religious ecstasy. It was ground very, very finely and mixed into milk with almonds, black pepper, lotus seeds, and aromatic herbs and sweetened with cane sugar.

Ayurvedic medicine used cannabis for the alleviation of migraine headaches and stomach spasms. An antispasmodic and anodyne for pain, it is known to promote digestion, increase appetite, and assist in the flow of urine. According to Naveen Patnaik this plant was honored as

> one of the precious things recovered at the birth of the universe from the primeval sea, and was taken by the king of the gods to gain immortality.

For some, cannabis can stimulate and enhance sexual experiences. It puts others right to sleep. But this herb can raise the sexual

experience of the sensually inclined to divine dimensions. It can amplify sexual sensations and enhance the sense of two being joined as one. An aphrodisiac confection made in Algiers consists of cannabis, sugar, cinnamon, cloves, cardamom, nutmeg, pine kernels, pistachios, and orange juice and peel, grated. In Morocco a mixture of cannabis, honey, and spices is called *majoon*. Eating cannabis can create even more exquisite erotic sensations than smoking it. A rich, emollient oil is extracted from the seeds, making a great lip balm or addition to massage oils.

Kava Kava (Piper methysticum)

A Polynesian root with dreamy, warm, euphoric qualities, kava kava can be sensually relaxing. It can actually be too relaxing for some, sending them to la-la-land, pleasantly inducing either a deep, dreamless sleep or vivid, erotic, exotic dreams. Kava kava is chewed fresh and honored as a sacrament in the Polynesian islands to welcome special guests and friends. For a hot drink try placing a small handful of the dried root in a little more than enough coconut milk to completely cover it and simmer until just hot. Or blend 1 ounce of kava kava powder with 10 ounces of coconut milk and 1 tablespoon of lecithin in a blender. You can add chopped fresh lemongrass for flavor and sweeten with a little cane or light brown sugar. Blend well. Let it sit for 20–30 minutes. Strain. Serve warm or cool. Serves 1 or 2.

Passionflower (Passiflora incarnata)

In spite of its name, passionflower does not tend to induce passion. But it is relaxing to the nerves and body when there is too much tension, thus helping to relax a person into their sensuality. Try it for insomnia. Passionflower combines well with skullcap leaves in equal parts as a tea or tincture. Use 1 heaping spoonful each of dry herb or 1/2 teaspoon each of the tincture for each cup of boiling water. Spearmint flavors the tea nicely.

Skullcap (Scutellaria sp.)

A nervine that is both relaxing to the mind and a tonic to the nerves, skullcap generally

Jean-Jules-Antoine Lecomte de Nouy, *The White Slave,* 1888. Oil on canvas. Musée des Beaux-Arts, Nantes, France.

"smooths the edges." It is magnesium-rich and is excellent for PMS, mood swings, or anytime a little attitude adjustment is needed. I call it "bitchwort." I had a couple come in to the shop where I was working to say, "Skullcap saved our marriage!" Skullcap can be taken as a tea or tincture. For tea, bring water to a rolling boil, pour 1 cup over 1–2 teaspoons of the leaves, and let steep for 5–10 minutes. For tincture, take ½ teaspoon as needed. It is pleasant combined with spearmint or lemongrass.

To Make a Tea

If the tea you want to make consists of flowers or leaves, the general directions are to use 1 heaping teaspoon for each cup of water. The water is boiled, taken off the heat, and poured onto the herb or blend of herbs. It is then covered and left to steep for about 7–10 minutes.

If seeds are to be added to tea, it is best to either crush them in a mortar with a pestle or grind them slightly to break through their outer hulls. The seeds do not need to be completely powdered.

If the tea you wish to make consists of roots or bark, the general directions are to use 1 heaping teaspoon for each cup of water. It is best to use an enamel or glass pan, since the herbs should not be cooked in metal. The herbs and cold water are combined and brought to a gentle simmer. With the heat on low, continue to simmer for about 10 minutes.

If you have a combination of roots and leaves, simmer the roots first. Take the pan off the heat, add the leaves, cover, let the mixture steep for 10 minutes, and then strain. Drink 1–3 cups a day.

To Make a Tincture

Combine the dried ingredients. Fill half of a clean 1-quart canning jar with the blend. Then completely cover the dried mixture of herbs with brandy or vodka and add a thumb's-width more of the alcohol. The next day check the level of the alcohol. The dried plants soak up some of it, so you may need to add more alco-

hol, to about 2 fingers'-width above the level of the herbs. Shake this each day for 3–4 weeks. As you shake your jar, think of your reproductive system as healthy and strong and be sure to thank the herbs. After 4 weeks strain the herbs through a few layers of cheesecloth. Squeeze out all the liquid with your hands. Compost the herbs and store your tincture in a dark bottle away from heat. A good dosage to start with is $1/2$ teaspoon of the tincture in a cup of hot tea, juice, or water. If you wish to, you may pour boiling water over the spoonful of tincture and let it sit for 5 minutes. About 75 percent of the alcohol will evaporate.

For more severe symptoms, work up to 1 teaspoon of the tincture 3 times a day.

To Make an Herbal Syrup

Make 2 cups of strong herbal tea using 1 cup of dried herbs for a quart of water. Steep flowers and leaves; gently simmer roots and bark. While the tea is still warm, add $1/2$ cup of honey and 2 tablespoons of vegetable glycerin. A quarter cup of brandy is optional. Store this in the refrigerator. To make into tea, use 3 or 4 tablespoons or more for each cup of hot, cold, or carbonated water.

Chapter 4

Aphrodisiac Foods
and Voluptuous Vittles

What foods do you find sensually stimulating?

Any foods that bear the remotest resemblance to the sex organs of women and men, as well as all sensuous fruits and foods, have been used to inspire sensuality and desire. Some favorites are almonds, apricots, artichokes, asparagus, bananas, beans, berries, carrots, chocolate, citrus fruits, creamy foods, corn, cucumbers, dates, eggs, figs, fish, edible flowers, garlic, grapes, mangoes, nuts, olives, onions, oysters, papayas, peaches, peas, persimmons, pine nuts, pomegranates, potatoes, and stuffed pasta shells and other stuffed foods. Figs, which symbolized the feminine, with their deep and opulent clefts resembling female genitalia, were consumed with lusty abandon at Greek love orgies.

Breads and cakes baked in the forms of male and female genitalia were very common in ancient Greece and Rome. In Rome they were called *coliphia* and *siligone* and were baked by prostitutes referred

> *Food is created by the sex of plants and animals.*
>
> Diane Ackerman

to as "baker's girls." It was the custom of these prostitutes to entertain their customers in the bake ovens—after they had cooled, of course. In Italy vulva cakes are blessed to ensure fertility of the women and special shaped cakes are blessed by the village priest during the Easter holy processions.

Hendrick Van Balen, *The Feast of Neptune,* seventeenth century.

A quaint custom among certain lusty medieval girls was to frolic naked in the wheat before grinding it into flour and baking it into cakes. Later a girl would offer a cake to her

beloved who, upon tasting the delectable morsel, was immediately lovestruck and possessed with a burning desire for the charms of its baker.

Young women wishing to seduce a lover would cover their bodies with honey, then roll in bread crumbs. These would then be rubbed off and shaped into little cakes that would be fed to the prospective lover. (Ah ha! Pheromones at work!)

I remember as a teenager coming home to celebrate my parents' anniversary, finding raw oysters waiting on the table with lemons, and thinking, "*This* is for dinner? Hey! Where's the pasta?" I immediately asked to go to a friend's house for dinner; I could not imagine eating those things. My parents nodded, Yes, go! It took me years to realize that they had planned it that way. They would feed each other the raw oysters drizzled with fresh, tangy lemon juice. It took me two decades before I was to try oysters. Then I ate seven oysters barbecued in lemon butter at one sitting. They slid right out of their little shells into my mouth. I chewed lightly, giggled, then swallowed those delicious, sensual, titillating creatures of the sea. Oh, yes. They work!

Remember to eat with your fingers! It is

*Oysters
are the most
tender and delicate
of all seafoods. They
stay in bed all day and
night. They never work or
take any exercise, are
stupendous drinkers and
wait for their meals to come
to them.*

Hector Bolitho,
The Glorious Oyster

very special to feed your beloved with your fingers. It is important also to allow yourself to be fed. For some reason the food tastes even better! Don't hold back—a food feast arising spontaneously can be a highly erotic experience, especially if you feast on one another.

You'd be surprised to discover that many sweetmeats, pastries and cakes, stuffed vegetables, and pastas often hold a dramatic resemblance to genitalia. Different cultures have their favorite pastries with evocative names, such as virgin's breasts, cannoli, spotted dick, hot cross buns, lips of the beauty, ladies' thighs, and nipples of Venus.

Favorite Seductive Foods for Finger-Licking Feasts
What a Dish—Soups, Appetizers, and Entrees

Blood-Orange Cold Soup or Sorbet

This shade of red is enough to feast the eyes upon, not to mention what it does to the taste buds.

13 blood oranges, juiced
³/₄ cup sugar
2 tablespoons Grand Marnier
2 tablespoons fresh lemon juice

Puree ingredients in a blender and chill for soup or freeze for a sorbet. Remove sorbet from the freezer before it is solid and use a spoon to shave or scrape it into goblets.

Fennel Soup

1-pound fennel bulb, chopped
1 cup white wine
1 cup prepared vegetable or chicken bouillon
Pine nuts, toasted, as garnish

Combine the ingredients in a saucepan. Simmer for 10 minutes and then puree in a blender. This may be served hot or chilled. Top the soup with toasted pine nuts.

Fresh fennel may be eaten like celery. In Italian it is called *finocchio*. Scoop a spoonful of ricotta cheese on the fresh stalk and sprinkle with cinnamon.

Breasts of the Green Goddess or Lingam Nut Log

A delicious and popular herbal cheese spread that is fun to shape! Bring it to the next adult pot luck.

2 8-ounce packages cream cheese, softened
$^1/_2$ cup pesto
$^1/_2$ cup chopped sundried tomatoes, rehydrated in a little hot water, then drained
$^1/_4$ cup toasted pine nuts
1 bunch chives, as garnish
Sundried tomato pieces, as garnish
Olives, as garnish

Mix cream cheese, pesto, chopped sundried tomatoes, and toasted pine nuts together well. With wet hands form into 2 breasts. Chop chives finely and pat over the breasts to make a green goddess. Decorate with 2 pieces of dried tomato with olives for nipples! Serve with crackers or bread. This recipe may also be shaped into a "log" with 2 balls at one end, then sprinkled with toasted chopped nuts.

Moroccan Chicken

1 large chicken, cut into pieces
$^1/_4$ cup butter
$^1/_4$ cup canola oil
1 teaspoon cinnamon
$^1/_4$ teaspoon each of turmeric, paprika, cumin, and cayenne
$^1/_2$ cup chopped, toasted almonds
$^1/_2$ cup raisins

Preheat the oven to 400°F.

Sprinkle salt and pepper on the chicken pieces. Melt the butter with the oil, add the spices, and use this mixture to baste the chicken while it is roasting until the juices run clear.

Serve over couscous cooked with chicken broth along with the almonds and raisins.

Sensuous Sicilian Chicken

This has been a favorite Sicilian way of preparing mouth-watering, tangy chicken since antiquity.

1/2 cup olive oil
1/2 cup lemon juice
2 pinches salt
1 whole chicken, cut into pieces
Parsley sprigs

Mix the olive oil, lemon juice, and salt together, pour over the chicken pieces, and marinate for a few hours or overnight. Cook the chicken on the grill, using a parsley brush (sprigs of parsley tied together with string) to baste it with the marinade until the thigh is cooked to the bone and very tender. This is excellent cold. It is my family's favorite Sunday chicken recipe.

Isis's Spiced Curry Chicken

1 teaspoon curry powder
1 cup plain yogurt
1 whole chicken, cut into chunks

Mix 1 teaspoon of curry powder into 1 cup of yogurt. Pour this over chunks of chicken and marinate for a few hours or overnight. Skewer the chicken chunks onto wooden sticks and grill until done. Finger-licking tasty.

> *Anything worth doing is worth doing slowly.*
>
> Mae West

Stuffed Pasta Shells

1 pound extra-large pasta shells
2 cups ricotta cheese
1 package frozen spinach, thawed and squeezed out
2 tablespoons pesto
1 pinch nutmeg
1 egg
1/3 cup grated romano cheese

Preheat oven to 350°F. Boil water, add pasta, and cook until shells are al dente. Mix ingredients together and stuff into pasta. Top with a spoonful of marinara sauce and more grated cheese. Bake covered in preheated oven for 25 minutes until heated through.

Stuffed Red Passion Peppers

4 medium to large red bell peppers

3 onions, sliced

3 cloves garlic

3 tablespoons olive oil

4 large tomatoes, seeded (or 1 can tomatoes)

$1/4$ cup currants, soaked in hot water and drained

3 cups cooked brown basmati rice

$1/2$ cup chopped parsley

$1/2$ cup pine nuts, toasted

$1/2$ cup chopped fresh mint

$1/2$ teaspoon salt

$1/2$ teaspoon red pepper flakes, optional

Preheat oven to 350°F.

Sauté onions and garlic in oil over medium heat for about 10 minutes. Add tomatoes and currants, simmer 5 minutes, and add the remaining ingredients, stirring well. Slice off the very top of the peppers, and clean them out scraping out the seeds and veins. Stuff peppers with the rice mixture and cover with the pepper top. Place in a baking dish with a cover, add a couple of splashes of wine or water to the baking dish, cover, and bake in preheated oven for $1/2$ hour. This pilaf is also good stuffed in cabbage or grape leaves but is equally delicious on its own.

Pasta Puttanesca

In Italian *pasta puttanesca* means "prostitute's pasta." It was very quickly and easily made between seeing clients!

Pasta of choice

Olive oil, to taste

Red chili peppers, to taste

Grated romano cheese, to taste

Cook pasta in boiling water, strain, and drizzle with olive oil, then sprinkle with red chili peppers and a generous handful of romano cheese. *Pronta e deliziosa!*

Green peas boiled carefully with onions and powdered with cinnamon, ginger, and cardamon create for the consumer amorous passion and strength in coitus.
Sheikh Nefzawi, *The Perfumed Garden*, sixteenth-century Arabian love manual

Flavored Butters or Ghee

These compound butters combine herbs and spices with liqueurs and nuts and may be spread on any type of toast, bread, muffin, bagel, scone, croissant, . . . or buns.

Chocolate Spiced Butter

1 stick softened butter or $1/2$ cup ghee
3 tablespoons cocoa
2–3 tablespoons honey
$1/2$ teaspoon cinnamon
$1/2$ teaspoon ground aniseed

Thoroughly mix ingredients together. Spread generously.

Orange Nut Butter

1 stick butter or $1/2$ cup ghee
$1/2$ cup finely ground toasted almonds or pecans
Zest of 1 orange
1 tablespoon brown sugar
4 drops orange essential oil or 1 teaspoon Grand Marnier
Chopped candied ginger, optional

Soften butter by grating it with a cheese grater. Use a fork to mash and stir in the rest of the ingredients. Pack into a pretty dish.

Honey Butter

1 stick softened butter
2–3 tablespoons honey
Optional flavorings:
  2 tablespoons orange liqueur
  2 tablespoons almond liqueur
  2 tablespoons vanilla extract
  Zest of citrus peel

Mix ingredients together and fluff with a fork. Use fingers to spread.

Rich Mocha Butter

1 stick softened butter
2 tablespoons honey
2 tablespoons cocoa powder
1 tablespoon instant espresso powder
2 tablespoons Kahlua or coffee liqueur

Use a fork to whip butter ad honey together. Gently fold in remaining ingredients.

Roasted Garlic Butter

1 stick softened butter
3 heads garlic, sliced $1/4$" from end
1 teaspoon red pepper flakes or $1/2$ teaspoon cayenne
1 tablespoon minced parsley leaf

Preheat oven to 350°F.

Wrap garlic heads in foil or parchment and roast for 1 hour in preheated oven. Remove from oven. When cooled, squeeze garlic into bowl with butter and pepper and mash with a fork, then add the minced parsley. Try this on baked potatoes.

Fruits and Nuts

These special gifts of nature that contain the very seeds of life have long been associated with fertility, abundance, lushness, and potency. Pine nuts and almonds were favored aphrodisiacs of the Romans and Arabs.

Warm Winter Fruit Compote

This is an iron-rich, nourishing compote perfect for starting or ending your day.

2 cups apple cider
1 cup dried apricots
1 cup dried pears
$1/4$ cup golden raisins
$1/2$ cup pitted prunes
$1/3$ cup apricot brandy
1 organic orange, sliced
2 tart green apples cut into chunks
2 or more slices fresh ginger
2 cinnamon sticks
1 bag frozen dark sweet cherries

Simmer together over low heat until apples are tender but still hold their shape. Serve warm. A dollop of vanilla yogurt on top is tasty.

Italian postcard.

If, my pet, you gave me these two apples as tokens of your breasts, I bless you for your great kindness. But if your gift does not go beyond the apples, you wrong me by refusing to quench the fierce fire you lit.

Silentiarius, sixth-century Greek poet

Cleopatra's Love Nuggets

This herbal candy was inspired by Rosemary Gladstar and can help keep your strength up during passionate play. It is rich in protein, calcium, and vitamin F.

1 cup raw sesame tahini
³/₄ cup honey
¹/₂ teaspoon each cinnamon, ginger, cardamom, and aniseed
2 tablespoons cocoa powder
1–2 teaspoons damiana cordial, vanilla extract, Amaretto, anisette, or rose water
Shredded coconut or cocoa powder for rolling
Optional additions:
  1 tablespoon finely chopped fresh mint leaves
  1 tablespoon powdered nettle leaves (powdered in a coffee or spice grinder)
  1 drop peppermint essential oil
  2 teaspoons grated orange peel
  5 drops orange oil

In a medium bowl, stir together tahini and honey. Add powdered herbs and flavorings and combine.

Roll mixture into balls (if too soft to shape, add more powdered herbs) and then roll to coat in shredded coconut or cocoa powder, or use as stuffing for dates.

Almond Paste or Marzipan

Almond paste can be colored and shaped into all sorts of erotic shapes. One or two teaspoons of rose water or liqueur may be added for variety. A drop or two of anise, orange, peppermint, spearmint, or lemon essential oils can be added to the water part of the recipe as a substitute for the almond extract.

2 cups whole almonds to be blanched
1 cup sugar
¹/₂ cup water
¹/₂ teaspoon vanilla
3 tablespoons light corn syrup
¹/₄ teaspoon almond extract
Powdered sugar, as needed

Preheat oven to 300°F.

To blanch the almonds, cover them with boiling water and soak for 5–10 minutes. The skins should now slip right off. Dry the almonds in the preheated oven for about 5 minutes. Before they cool off, grind them in the food processor with 2 tablespoons of the sugar until powdery. Add the remaining sugar, water, vanilla, corn syrup, and almond extract and process until the paste is very smooth. Dust a marble slab or board with powdered sugar, place the combined mixture on it, and knead briefly. This makes an ambrosial stuffing for dates.

You may want to substitute a tablespoon of rose water for the water or, when kneading the almond paste, try adding a few drops of beet juice to give a rosy color. Grate the raw beets and squeeze the juice through cheesecloth for desired shade. Another variation is to add grated orange peel, with 1 tablespoon of orange flower water substituted for part of the water in the recipe.

For added decadence, balls of almond paste may be dipped in chocolate using a toothpick. Let these dry on waxed paper.

Sesame Seeds

Sesame cakes and candies have long been served at wedding banquets as a fructifying influence. Tahini, raw sesame butter, is a rich source of calcium, vitamin E, vitamin F, and protein. It contains beneficial oils for the hair and skin and nourishes the body. Cleopatra knew the benefits of this prized food. She wore it well.

Sophisticates often insert into the vagina fruits such as strawberries or cherries, or an orange section or an apple slice dipped in honey, thereupon sucking or drawing them out again, and eating them with much enjoyment. The banana is classically used in this way. Not to be done by persons with false teeth.

G. Legman, *Oragenitalism,* 1969

Peaches or Raspberries in a Vanilla–Red Wine Sauce

Made from fresh, fragrant fruits of summer soaked in a sweet wine marinade, this is an old Sicilian dish that announced summer was upon us. I still love sipping the wine left over in the bowl.

Ripe peaches or raspberries
Brown sugar
Red wine
Vanilla extract
Rose water or orange flower
    water, optional

Slice fresh ripe peaches or raspberries into a bowl. Sprinkle lightly with brown sugar and drizzle red wine and a spoon of vanilla extract over the top as you would a dressing. Stir well, scooping the wine over the fruit. A spoon of rose water or orange flower water may be added for variation.

Still Life, Edward Ladell, 1821–1886.

Candied Citrus

These delectable, mouth-watering morsels may be used in baking or served as part of a sweetmeat platter.

Use 3 grapefruits, 7 or 8 thick-skinned oranges, or 6 or 7 lemons. Organic citrus is recommended.

Citrus fruits of choice
3 cups sugar
1½ cups water
3 tablespoons light corn syrup

Peel the citrus or slice and pull out the fruit. Put the peels in a large pot of water, bring to a boil, and simmer for 20–25 minutes. Drain the water and let the peels cool down enough to handle. Use a spoon and scrape away the white pith. Slice or cut the peels into narrow strips.

Stir together the water, sugar, and corn syrup in a nonaluminum 3-quart pan, stirring until it boils. When the syrup is clear add the peels, lower the heat, and slowly cook for about 1 hour until they look translucent. With a slotted spoon scoop out the peels and drain on a rack. Store in the refrigerator if you are using them for baking. To serve as a sweetmeat, first drain and then roll the peels in a little sugar.

Let them dry for 2 hours.

The candied peels may also be dipped in chocolate. Melt 6 ounces of semisweet chocolate chips with a spoonful of sweet butter. Holding one end of the peel, dip half of it in the chocolate, then set on waxed paper to dry.

Naranjas y Limones, and Chiquita Piconera, Julio Romero de Torres, 1874–1930.

Glazed Nuts: An Old Favorite Family Recipe

These scrumptious nuts may be served as part of a sweetmeat dessert platter.

> 3 cups lightly toasted nuts—almonds, pecans, or walnuts (or a combination)
> 1 cup brown sugar
> 1 tablespoon butter
> 1 tablespoon milk
> 1/2 teaspoon cinnamon
> 2 teaspoons grated orange peel or 4 drops orange essential oil

Cook the sugar, butter, milk, and cinnamon over low heat until bubbly. Stir well into nuts with orange peel or orange oil and spread on waxed paper to cool and dry. Store in an airtight container. Serve Glazed Nuts either broken up or in clusters.

Tantric Trail Mix

For a great energy booster try mixing a handful of raw pumpkin seeds with a pinch each of cardamom, ginger, and cinnamon and a handful of raisins. This mix is rich in zinc, iron, protein, and vitamin F.

Spicy Nuts

> 2 1/2 cups nuts
> 2 tablespoons oil
> 1/2 teaspoon ground cumin
> 1/4 teaspoon ground cayenne
> 1 teaspoon sugar
> 1/2 teaspoon salt

Preheat oven to 300°F.

Heat oil and spices in a skillet for 15 seconds, stirring in the sugar and salt. Pour this mixture over the nuts in a bowl. Stir to coat. Then spread on a baking sheet.

Bake in preheated oven for 20 minutes until toasted. Cool. Store in an airtight container.

> *He who feels that he is weak for coition should drink before going to bed a glassful of very thick honey and eat twenty almonds and one hundred kernels of the pine tree. He must follow this regime for three nights.*
> Sheikh Nefzawi, *The Perfumed Garden,* sixteenth-century Arabian love manual

Elisabeth's Paté Majik

1 cup almonds
1 cup pitted dates
Juice and zest of 1 orange
$^1/_2$ teaspoon cinnamon
$^1/_2$ cup toasted coconut
1 large pinch cannabis, optional

Soak the almonds overnight in water. Drain the next day and put in a processor with the pitted dates, the orange juice and zest, cinnamon, coconut, and cannabis. Process until well mixed. Shape into small balls or serve over sliced fruit with a dollop of yogurt.

Aphrodite's Nipples

These nippy tidbits are made with dried figs and sesame. Other dried fruits or ground seeds such as pumpkin or sunflower may be substituted according to taste.

1 pound black mission figs
$^3/_4$ cup sesame seeds, lightly toasted
Juice and zest of 1 organic orange or 5
    drops orange oil
3 drops anise oil
1 tablespoon vanilla extract
$^1/_2$ teaspoon cinnamon or cardamom

$^1/_4$ teaspoon cayenne pepper
Sugar or cocoa, as garnish

Remove stems from the figs and soften figs by lightly steaming them. Put figs in a food processor with the toasted sesame seeds, the orange juice and zest (or orange oil), the anise oil, vanilla extract, cinnamon or cardamom, and cayenne pepper. Process to a paste. Roll into large nipples. Dust with sugar or cocoa.

Sweetmeats

As a student of oriental dance I have long been fascinated with the women of the harem, their dances, and their lives. These women made delectable sherbets with rose petals or jasmine and orange blossoms and fed them to one another along with sweetmeats such as stuffed dates, glazed spiced nuts, and candied citrus peels. All of these can be nibbled either as dessert or to give you more energy during lovemaking.

Pitted dates sprinkled with rose water, stuffed with cream cheese, and sprinkled with coconut are my favorites! I dye the coconut a fuschia pink with fresh, finely grated beetroot squeezed through cheesecloth and then mixed in a bowl to color the coconut.

maiden, which she had plucked herself from a branch, that was as supple as her own body. And sweet it was to place my hand upon it as though it was the breast of the one who gave it. Pure was the fragrance of the apple, like the breath of the giver. One could see the color of her cheek on it, and I thought I was tasting her lips when I began to eat the apple.

The Kama Sutra

Other good stuffings for pitted dates, prunes, and figs are almond paste (marzipan) scented with orange blossom water or rose water, sesame tahini with honey and grated orange peel, glazed nuts, Nutella, and chocolate chips. Use your imagination. If you surround yourselves with these delicacies in the bedroom, you won't have to keep running back and forth to the kitchen.

Garden of Eden Salad

The apple which I received from the hand of the most charming, gazelle-like

$^1/_2$ cup vanilla yogurt (or mayonaise)
1 tablespoon honey
Zest of $^1/_2$ orange
$^1/_2$ teaspoon cinnamon
$^1/_2$ teaspoon cardamom
3 large red apples, diced
$^1/_2$ cup chopped toasted nuts
$^1/_4$ cup raisins
$^3/_4$ cup diced celery
Chopped candied ginger, optional
Crumbled blue cheese, optional
1 spoonful of rose water, optional

Combine yogurt, honey, zest, and spices. Pour over apples, nuts, raisins, and celery. Stir well. Sprinkle with candied ginger, blue cheese, or rose water if desired.

Refreshing Orange Mint Salad

3 or 4 oranges
12 spearmint leaves, thinly sliced
1 cup jicama root, peeled and diced
1 tablespoon olive oil
2 pinches salt
Black pepper to taste

Peel and section the oranges. Slice the sections into bite-sized pieces. Make a chiffonade of the spearmint by stacking 8–10 leaves on top of each other and cutting very close into shreddy slices. Combine the orange pieces, spearmint, and diced jicama in a bowl and drizzle a tablespoon of olive oil over the salad with 2 pinches of salt and some black pepper. Toss gently and serve.

After a perfect meal
we are more susceptible
to the ecstasy
of love
than at any other time.
Dr. Hans Balzi

Watermelon Sorbet

This tasty sorbet is refreshing and beautiful, especially on hot summer nights.

1 can coconut milk
$1/2$ cup sugar
6 cups pureed red watermelon (5–6 pounds watermelon)
$1/4$ cup lemon juice
1 tablespoon rose water or orange flower water, optional

Dissolve the sugar in the coconut milk. When it is cool, add the pureed red watermelon and the lemon juice. A tablespoon of either rose water or orange flower water may be added to perfume the sorbet. Pour this into a 9" x 13" baking dish, freeze, thaw slightly, then beat with beaters or shave into goblets.

Sweet Indulgences

Breast or Phallic Cookies

This is the basic butter cookie recipe, dough to be shaped as desired according to your imagination. These melt in the mouth. A half cup of chopped toasted pecans may be added if you wish.

    1 cup softened butter
    1 cup powdered sugar
    1 egg, beaten
    1½ teaspoons vanilla (anise flavoring or
       Amaretto liqueur may be substituted)
    2½ cups flour, sifted
    ½ cup pecans, chopped and toasted,
       optional
    Powdered sugar, as garnish

Preheat oven to 350°F.

Cream butter and sugar until light and fluffy. Add egg and mix well, blend in the flour and vanilla, and form into assorted shapes. Be creative! Bake in preheated oven for 9 minutes or until lightly browned. Sift powdered sugar over the warm cookies if desired.

Mocha Magic Sauce

    12 ounces semisweet chocolate chips
    3–4 tablespoons whipping cream
    2 tablespoons vanilla extract or liqueur
    1–2 tablespoons instant espresso dissolved
       in cream

Melt the chocolate in a double boiler or in a pan over boiling water. Thin with the cream, liqueur, and espresso. Serve warm. Wonderful for dipping fingers in . . . among other things.

Garlic Goddess Celebration

Here is a unique blend of aphrodisiacs for garlic lovers.

Steam a handful of whole garlic cloves until tender or until a toothpick inserts easily. Place on a paper towel to absorb moisture. When they are dry, stick a toothpick in each clove and dip into the above chocolate recipe. Let them cool. Surprise!

The greatest pleasure in life is doing what people say you cannot do.

Walter Bagehot

Oasis Bars

These scrumptious sweetmeat-like bars have been a favorite sensuous flavor and texture combination of mine for many years. This is a tactile recipe, so you'll need to have clean hands ready.

½ cup butter
¼ cup light honey
1⅓ cups whole wheat pastry flour
¼ teaspoon salt
2 teaspoons vanilla extract
2½ cups pitted dates
¾ cup coconut
1½ cups broken walnuts or pecans
1 egg, beaten
1 teaspoon baking powder

Preheat oven to 325°F.

For the crust: Cream together the butter and the light honey. Add the whole wheat pastry flour, the salt, and 1 teaspoon of the vanilla extract. Mix this with a fork, then squish it together with your hands and press the crust mixture into an 8" x 12" baking dish. Bake in preheated oven for 20 minutes.

For the topping: In a large bowl, squish together the soft pitted dates. (The barhi or soft black dates are great for this recipe.) Add the coconut, broken walnuts or pecans, beaten egg, remaining teaspoon of vanilla extract, and baking powder.

Spread this mixture evenly on top of the cooled crust. Return to preheated oven and bake 20 minutes more. Let cool before slicing into bars.

Cinnamon Rum Balls

Delicious little spiced balls to nibble on. These really taste better when they have aged a couple of weeks.

2 cups graham cracker crumbs
2 tablespoons cocoa powder
1 heaping teaspoon cinnamon
2 teaspoons grated orange rind
1 cup sifted powdered sugar
⅓ cup light rum, vanilla extract, Grand Marnier, or orange liqueur
Cocoa powder and powdered sugar for rolling, optional

Mix all ingredients and form into small balls. Roll balls in additional powdered sugar or cocoa powder. Place them in an airtight tin or jar and let them sit away from heat for 10 days. Enjoy as finger food.

Chocolate-Dipped Strawberries and Dried Apricots

This is truly a botanical marriage made in heaven, combining mouth-watering fruits with seductive dark chocolate.

Slowly and carefully melt 1 package of semisweet chocolate chips in a double boiler or in a saucepan set over a pan of water. Stir and heat until melted, keeping the chocolate on a medium-low heat, as it can curdle if it gets too hot. A small amount of milk may be added to thin the chocolate. Dip the strawberries and apricots (cherries, apple and banana slices, and/or orange slices may also be dipped) in the warm chocolate, making sure that the fruit is not wet; if it is, pat it dry. Place the dipped fruit on parchment or waxed paper until the chocolate has firmed up. A toothpick may come in handy to help with the dipping of some fruits. These fruit confections may be placed in the refrigera-

The best way to behave is to misbehave.
Mae West

tor to cool. During the winter months when some fresh fruits are not in season, dried fruits such as Turkish or regular apricots, mangoes, papayas, peaches, pears, or candied ginger may be used for dipping.

Rich Melt-in-Your-Mouth Aromatic Chocolate Mousse

This luscious, smooth mousse is excellent to use as a fruit dip and a finger dip. Try it as an edible body paint!

    6 ounces semisweet chocolate chips
    1 ounce unsweetened chocolate, chopped
    2 tablespoons Amaretto (or Grand
        Marnier or vanilla extract)
    2 tablespoons water (or rose water or
        orange blossom water)
    4 eggs, separated
    1 cup whipping cream

Melt the chocolate with the liqueur or vanilla extract and water in a double boiler or in a pan over water. Stir until it is well melted and smooth. Remove from the heat and cool slightly.

Meanwhile, whip the cream until it holds a soft shape.

Whisk the egg yolks into the chocolate.

Warm the egg whites over a bowl of hot water until they are almost warm. In a separate bowl, beat the whites until soft peaks form. Fold half of the whites into the chocolate mixture, then fold in the remaining whites and the whipped cream. Pour this into goblets, a serving bowl, or a piecrust. Chill before serving.

Passion-in-Paradise White Chocolate Sauce

This is truly heavenly for white-chocolate lovers. Used as a dipping sauce for fruits and fingers, it also makes a good, edible, white body paint to drizzle on those special dessert areas that deserve extra attention. Try a few drops of the botanical colors to change the shades of the paint.

    10 ounces quality white chocolate
    5 ounces heavy cream
    2 tablespoons Grand Marnier (or
        Amaretto or vanilla extract)

Gently melt the chocolate with the cream over a pan of boiling water, stirring until smooth, then stir in the liqueur or vanilla extract. This is appealing warm or cooled.

La Torta Decadenza

In honor of the goddess of decadence, this rich chocolate cake has made it to many a birthday celebration.

10 ounces semisweet chocolate chips or
    pieces
2 sticks butter
5 large eggs
$1^1/_4$ cups sugar
$1/_3$ cup flour
$1^1/_2$ teaspoons baking powder
Optional flavorings:
    $1/_2$ teaspoon orange oil
    Zest from 1 large organic orange
    1 tablespoon Amaretto or Anisette
    1 teaspoon cinnamon
Powdered sugar

Preheat oven to 325°F.

Butter and flour a 10" spring-form pan. Stir the chocolate and butter in a heavy saucepan over low heat until melted and smooth. Beat the eggs and the sugar in a large bowl until they are well blended and start to thicken. Sift the flour and baking powder over the eggs and fold in. Then gradually fold in the chocolate mixture. Add one of the optional flavorings if desired. Scoop the batter into the prepared pan.

Bake in preheated oven for 20 minutes. Then cover the pan with foil and bake about 25–30 minutes longer, until an inserted toothpick comes out with moist crumbs attached. Remove from oven, uncover the cake, and cool on a rack. The cake will fall as it cools. Once cool, loosen the edges and release the side of the pan. Place a paper doily on top of the cooled cake and sift powdered sugar over it. Carefully remove the doily to reveal a beautiful snowflake design.

Sweet Cheese

1 quart vanilla whole-milk yogurt
$1/_2$ teaspoon cinnamon
$1/_2$ cup chopped dates or dried apricots
1 tablespoon honey

Place vanilla whole-milk yogurt in a triple layer of cheesecloth. Tie off with a rubber band and hang over a bowl overnight to drip out the whey. The liquid is like acidophilus milk and is delicious to sip. Open the cheesecloth the next morning and put the "cheese" in a bowl with cinnamon, chopped dates or dried apricots, and a tablespoon of honey. Mix it all together and use as a spread on nut bread or raisin bread or dollop on top of apple slices.

Apricot Cream Dream

    2 cups whipping cream
    1 8-ounce jar apricot preserves or jam

Whip cream until stiff and stir in apricot preserves or jam. This makes a good edible body cream or topping for your favorite dessert.

Aromatic Whipped Cream

    $1/2$ pint whipping cream
    1–2 drops essential oil, neroli or rose
      geranium
    2 teaspoons sugar

Combine ingredients and whip together. Use as a topping for dessert, a dip for fruit, or an edible decoration for your breasts.

Botanical Food Colorings

Here are some botanical solutions for getting luscious colors into your gastronomic delights. Try freezing these liquid colors in ice-cube trays to have on hand for impulsive use later on.

These natural food colorings may be used to dye shredded coconut or buttercream frosting. Squeeze drops of color onto the dried coconut in a bowl and work the color in with a fork. Spread the colorful coconut out on paper towels to dry. Store in a jar away from light.

- For **magenta rose** grate fresh raw beets into cheesecloth.
- For **saffron gold** mix $1/4$ teaspoon of turmeric powder with 1 tablespoon of hot water. Stir with a chopstick and add 2 or 3 drops of orange oil and a pinch or two of sugar or a small drizzle of honey.
- For **sunset orange** start with the saffron-gold color and add drops of beet juice for the desired shade of orange.
- For **forest green** use liquid chlorophyll (found at a natural foods store) for a rich, deep green or 2 chlorophyll tablets crushed with a spoonful of warm water. A drop of spearmint or peppermint essential oil may be added as well.
- For **purple passion** use 1 tablespoon of Seneca unsweetened frozen grape-juice concentrate for a royal purple color.

Edible Flowers

Beautiful flowers can be used to decorate foods and drinks or frozen into ice cubes. Make sure the flowers you pick have not been sprayed. *Caution:* Not all flowers are edible. Please check a good field guide to flowers (or other reliable source) before eating any flowers. Among my favorite edibles are roses, borage, carnations, chive blossoms, nasturtiums, apple, orange, lemon, plum blossoms, rose geranium blossoms, gladiolas, fuschias, hibiscus, violets, violas, Johnny-jump-ups, lavender, passionflowers, poppies, rosemary flowers, squash blossoms, and calendula petals.

Check out your local nursery; many of these flowers can be grown easily. I decorate cheesecakes with flowers and add mint and fuzzy fennel leaves on the edges. A small handful of lavender flowers steeped in a pitcher of lemonade for a few hours is refreshing and delightful.

Crystallized Petals and Leaves

Crystallized or candied flowers, aromatic leaves, and herbs were popular during the Victorian era. Any of the edible blossoms, especially violets and rose petals, spearmint, peppermint, lemon verbena, lemon balm, or bergamot mint leaves may be candied or crystallized. They make a beautiful, toothsome addition to a special-occasion cake or cheesecake.

To gather leaves or flowers, pick them on a dry, sunny day. They may be brushed off with a small paintbrush used only for food. Beat an egg white until foamy and add $1/2$ tablespoon of water. Using the same small paintbrush or a clean finger, smooth the egg white over the entire flower or leaf. Surfaces should be moist but with no excess egg white. Dust the blossom on both sides with superfine granulated sugar. Shake off any excess sugar and place petals or leaves on waxed or parchment paper on a plate to dry.

For quick drying, leave the plate of flowers in your car on a warm day, with the windows rolled up. They may also be placed in the oven with just the pilot light on or in an oven that has been on its lowest setting, then turned off.

Chapter 5

Libidinous Libations:
Thirst-Quenching, Revitalizing, and Refreshing Beverages

Alcohol

As I write this chapter I am sipping a jade cordial glass of Godet's Belgian White Chocolate Liqueur. *Smooooooth.*

Alcohol, the product of a naturally occurring process, has long been used to extract and preserve the beneficial, healing properties of herbs and spices. A small amount can warm up the coldest of feet by increasing circulation.

Taken in small amounts, alcohol may reduce anxiety and inhibitions and increase the libido, but too much too often has just the opposite effect. A depressant, it can cause a decrease in arousal, pleasure, erection, and orgasm if drunk to excess, so sip it slowly and make a little go a long way. Too much can wither your bits and make you willing but not able.

> *I can resist everything except temptation.*
> Oscar Wilde

Atholl Brose

Famous since 1475, this drink of whiskey traditionally mixed with honey or meal is named for the district in Scotland. Here is Wilma Carson's version of this Scottish whiskey–oatmeal tincture.

3 heaping tablespoons Scottish oatmeal
2 tablespoons honey (heather honey is
    traditional)
Approximately 2 cups water
Whiskey, to make up to 4 cups

Put oatmeal in a bowl and mix with water until you have a thick paste. Let it stand $^1/_2$ hour. Press it through a fine strainer, pressing down with a spoon so that the oatmeal is quite dry. Compost the oatmeal and mix the liquid with the honey. Stir with a silver spoon until blended. Pour into a quart bottle and fill up with whiskey. Cork well and always shake well before using. A fine dessert can be made by pouring 4 tablespoons of the oat drink into tall glasses and topping it with whipped cream. Serve chilled. Sprinkle with lightly toasted oatmeal.

Chocolate Cordial

I came up with this one premenstrual evening as I was craving that chocolate-covered cherry flavor.

$^1/_2$ cup brandy
1 cup Cocoa Syrup (page 87) or Hershey's
    chocolate syrup, dark or regular
2–3 drops almond extract or 1 teaspoon
    vanilla extract

Bottle the ingredients and shake well. Let sit for 2 days to 1 week. It will get smoother and silkier the longer it sits. It is tantalizing served over ice cream and fresh fruit and exquisite over sliced fresh peaches with toasted almonds. Use your lover's belly button as a cordial cup to sip this from.

Vivacious Vanilla Cordial

From the Latin *cor* meaning heart, a cordial was originally shared to bring heart to a friendship or situation. The heart is at the core. This vanilla cordial is delectable drizzled on fruit salads or just sipped.

To make vanilla cordial, add 2 tablespoons of honey to $^1/_2$ cup of prepared vanilla extract (see next paragraph). Stir to dissolve and add 1 tablespoon of water or rose water.

To make your own vanilla extract: Soak 2 vanilla beans for every ounce of brandy. (Make sure to split the beans lengthwise to let their essence out.) Soak the beans for 4 weeks. There you have it—vanilla extract. Sweetened with sugar or honey as above, you've made your own vanilla cordial.

Elder Flower Fizz

The fresh elder flowers should be picked on a sunny day when all the pollen is in the flowers. Each spring I double the batch, and it still runs out too soon! A delicately flavored flower fizz— if left to sit in a warm place, it turns into a potent sparkling wine.

5 quarts water
3^1/$_2$ cups turbinado sugar
Zest and juice of 1 organic lemon
2 tablespoons cider vinegar
13 elder flower heads

Boil the water and pour into a sterilized container. I use a ceramic crock. Add the turbinado sugar. (The flavor of honey can overpower the delicate elder scent.) Stir to dissolve the sugar.

When it is cool add the lemon juice and zest, the cider vinegar, and the elder flower heads. Cover this with several layers of cheesecloth and leave it for 24 hours.

Filter it into strong bottles with latch-down lids. It should be ready after 3 weeks of fizzing, after which it should be kept chilled. But I have let it go a little longer because its taste after 3 weeks was still too sweet. Then it started turning into a delicious wine with a kick—a sensuous slice of spring captured in a bottle.

Damiana Cordial

This is an old recipe of unknown origin. It has been a favorite at workshops and manages to show up at most herb-school functions. I found a bottle I had made three years before and had forgotten. The flavor and consistency were smooth, sippable, and luscious.

1 ounce damiana leaves
2 cups vodka or brandy
1^1/$_2$ cups springwater
1 cup honey
Vanilla extract or rose water, optional

Soak damiana leaves in vodka or brandy for 5 days.

After 5 days, strain and reserve the liquid in a bottle. Soak the alcohol-drenched leaves in the springwater for 3 days. Strain, reserve water, and compost the damiana leaves. Gently warm the water extract and dissolve the honey into it. Combine both of the extracts (water and alcohol) and stir well. Pour into a clean bottle and let sit 1 month or longer. It definitely gets better with age, like we do! Vanilla extract or rose water may be added for variety.

A couple of tablespoons of this cordial added to orange juice can spice up a weekend brunch. A quickie version of this would be to soak a few tablespoons of dried damiana leaves in a cup of commercially prepared vanilla extract for 2 days, strain, then sweeten with honey or maple syrup with a splash of rose water. Whichever you choose, shake well—it is ready to be sipped.

Herbed and Spiced Wines

Wines are one traditional way of preserving and taking herbal remedies, changing with the seasons as the available herbs dictate. White wines with flower petals, leaves, and fresh fruit are steeped, then sipped in the spring and summer. As cooler seasons arrive, hearty red wines are heated with roots, spices, bark, and dried fruits. Let each season be an inspiration to you with its bounty of abundant fruits and herbs.

For the wine recipes given here, any combination of the spices, flowers, or herbs mentioned may be used. Steep $1/2$ cup in each liter of wine in the refrigerator if using leaves and flowers; simmer very gently over low heat if using roots and barks. The wine may be sweetened with a light honey, sugar, or maple syrup. It may also be sweetened with licorice root or a pinch of stevia leaf.

Wine

Angelica Root (Angelica archangelica)

Angelica root was used in liqueurs in the eighteenth century to help women "warm up."

$1/2$ cup chopped dried angelica root
$1/2$ cup honey
1 liter wine, red or white

Steep dried angelica root and honey in wine for 2 weeks, shaking daily, then strain and sip from small glasses or add to hot water as an instant tea.

Fresh angelica root may be sliced thinly and mixed in a jar of honey, stirred until the air bubbles are gone. This should sit 2 weeks or more. Candied angelica root is used to decorate cakes in Europe.

Acqua fresca, vino puro, fica stretta, cazzo duro!

The proverbial
Italian necessities of life

Damiana Love Libations: Spiced Tea and Wine

1 cup dried damiana leaves
1/2 cup dried spearmint leaves
1/2 cup dried, fragrant, organic roses
1 tablespoon licorice root pieces
1 tablespoon cinnamon chips
1 tablespoon whole cloves
1 tablespoon ginger root pieces
Water or wine, as desired

Combine all ingredients except wine or water and mix together. Store the blend in a jar.

For tea, use 1 heaping teaspoon of blend per cup of boiling water. Steep about 5–7 minutes.

Or, for spiced wine, place the dried mixture in wine. Use 1/2 cup of the blend to 1 liter of wine. Steep in the refrigerator for 1 week.

Men and women of Imperial Rome would gather at the balnea mista (mixed bath), shed their togas, and leap with unabandoned glee into bubbly pools of champagne.

Greg and Beverly Frazier,
Aphrodisiac Cookery, Ancient & Modern

Mulled Vanilla Spiced Wine

May wine is made to celebrate May Day and the coming of spring by steeping dried sweet woodruff leaves and flowers in white wine. This is an old European favorite. Try lemon verbena leaves or pineapple sage leaves in a white or blush wine. Fresh or dried fruit may be added for flavor. I like using dried fruits in red wine and fresh fruits and berries in white or blush wine.

1/2 cup cinnamon pieces
1/4 cup ginger
2 tablespoons cloves
1/4 cup dried orange peel
2 tablepoons allspice berries
1/4 cup vanilla extract
2 tablespoons star anise, optional
2 small packets instant dried ginseng tea
   (found at herb shops and in
   Chinatowns)

Add the above ingredients to wine or juice and warm gently for 20–30 minutes. Strain before serving. This will warm the coldest of toes and other places.

Rose Wine

Take a bottle of your favorite wine (the blush wines are nice for this). My favorites are mead or honey wine. Steep a handful of very fragrant dried roses in the wine and store in a jar in the refrigerator for 2 days. Strain the roses out. Add another handful of dried roses to the same jar of wine and steep it again for 2 more days. Strain the flowers. Be sure to use unsprayed roses.

A quick way to make rose wine is to take a liter of wine and pour about $1/3$ cup of the wine into a glass. Drink it. Then add $1/3$ cup of

French postcard of the 1920s.

distilled rose water to the remaining wine. Shake it; it is now ready to enjoy. This makes a great gift.

Wine was the most popular drink among the city dwellers of Rome and Byzantium, while highly spiced beer was the favorite of the rural peasants. Honey wine, also known as mead, was made to celebrate the fertility of the spring and summer seasons. Raw honey, full of spring pollen, was mixed with rainwater and fermented into wine. Today, mead may be found at specialty liquor stores.

Red Wine Syrup

Imagine a berry or peach shortcake with this as a topping. This also makes a refreshing beverage when added to carbonated water—or add boiling water and try it hot.

2 cups red wine
2/3 cup sugar
2 tablespoons orange zest
1 bay leaf
1/4 teaspoon ground black pepper
1 tablespoon lemon juice

Boil wine, sugar, zest, bay leaf, and pepper for about 10 minutes, strain, and add lemon juice.

Sangria

This is a wine cooler with a punch to it. Serve it in small glasses or you could end up with overnight guests. (On the other hand, that could be fun.)

1 bottle of wine—red, blush, or white
1/3 cup brandy or orange liqueur
1/4 cup sugar or honey
1 orange, sliced
Juice of 1 orange
Sparkling mineral water or orange sherbet

In a large pitcher combine the wine, brandy or orange liqueur, sugar or honey, orange slices, and orange juice. Stir and add either a cup of sparkling mineral water with some ice or scoops of orange sherbet as desired.

Choosing, John William Godward, 1861–1922.

Summer-of-Love Passion Punch

This nectarous aromatic punch has been a memorable, sensuous influence at all kinds of gatherings.

1 12-ounce can frozen pink lemonade
2 cups fresh or frozen strawberries
1 bottle of wine, white zinfandel or blush
1/4 cup rose water
Fresh edible flowers, as garnish

Blend the strawberries with the lemonade and a cup or so of the wine. Puree the mixture, pour into a punch bowl, and add the remaining wine and the rose water. Garnish with fresh edible flowers. This punch may be semifrozen into a slushy ice drink.

Peach Blossom Punch

1/2 cup water
1/3 cup sugar
4 cups diced peaches
1 tablespoon lemon juice
1/4 cup Marsala wine
1 tablespoon orange blossom water

Heat the water and sugar to boiling to dissolve the sugar and simmer uncovered for 3 minutes to make a sugar syrup. Place the diced peaches and lemon juice in a food processor and whirl until smooth. Combine the Marsala wine, sugar syrup, and orange blossom water in a bowl and place in the freezer until partially frozen, stirring regularly. Scoop and serve in beautiful stemmed glasses.

Vino d'Amore (Wine of Love)

This sherry may be heated and sipped hot or all of the ingredients may be placed in a jar and steeped at room temperature for a week. It may also be enjoyed chilled.

1 bottle of sherry
1/4 cup honey or sugar
Juice of 1 orange
Grated peel of 1 orange
3 tablespoons vanilla extract (see page 79 to make your own)
3 inches of cinnamon stick

Combine all the ingredients in a saucepan and heat almost to boiling. Serve hot in mugs with a dollop of whipped cream. Makes enough for 8 servings.

Exquisite Elixirs

Cocoa Syrup

I was inspired to create my own chocolate syrup one night when it was too late to go to the store. This may be used in making your own soda fountain drinks or added to coffee.

    $1/3$ cup cocoa powder, sifted
    1 heaping cup sugar
    1 cup boiling water
    1 tablespoon vanilla extract

Mix the cocoa powder and sugar together and add the boiling water to dissolve the sugar. When cooled, add the vanilla extract.

Chocolate Nectar Soda

First make chocolate nectar syrup by mixing 2 cups of chocolate syrup with 1 tablespoon of orange flower water and 1 teaspoon of vanilla extract in a bottle. Use $1/4$ cup of this nectar to 2 tablespoons of cream in an 8-ounce glass and fill the glass with carbonated water.

Ginger Syrup

This is a simple recipe using fresh gingerroot. It was given to me by a student years ago and a bottle of it can always be found in my refrigerator. Ginger helps the circulation and brings warmth to the lower part of the body. Its spiciness and heat has been known to bring on hot flashes!

    This syrup may be added to hot water for a spicy hot beverage or to fizzy water with a squeeze of lemon and ice for your own home-made ginger ale.

    2 cups unpeeled ginger root
    4 cups water
    $1/2$ cup maple syrup or honey

Slice the unpeeled gingerroot, add to the water, and bring to a gentle simmer for $1/2$ hour. Strain the ginger pieces, then add the maple syrup or honey. Store this syrup in the refrigerator. For a refreshing beverage, use about $1/4$ cup syrup to a large glass of water. For extra flavor, a little lemon or orange juice may be added to your cup.

Rose or Orange Flower Love Syrup

This syrup can be added to a number of liquids to create a love seltzer, love wine, or love syrup.

 ¹/₂ cup light honey
 ¹/₂ cup rose water or orange blossom water

Warm the light honey very gently, then add either rose water or orange blossom water, stirring until completely incorporated. A couple of tablespoons may be added to carbonated mineral water as a seltzer or to juice, tea, or wine. You can also drizzle it over cakes or pastries.

Mints

Spearmint and peppermint have long been used as aphrodisiac favorites. Both mints are great added to fruit salads and as hot or cold tea. Try steeping handfuls of fresh mint in cold water overnight in the refrigerator. This is known as a cold infusion. It is very delicately perfumed and is beautiful as a tea, face wash, and hair rinse. A large handful of spearmint or peppermint added to a pitcher of lemonade is refreshing and revitalizing. A cold-weather favorite is to make a cup of peppermint tea using 2 peppermint tea bags instead of one. Pour on the hot water, steep 5 minutes, and sweeten with honey. Squeeze a little lemon and add 2 tablespoons of brandy. This warms the toes from the inside out. The mint leaves may be crystallized.

Resplendent Red Tea

 1 quart water at room temperature
 1 cup dried red hibiscus flowers
 Maple syrup, optional
 ¹/₄ cup rose water or orange flower water,
  optional

Pour the water over the dried red hibiscus flowers. Steep at room temperature for a couple of

L'Art et La Vie, Walter Crane, 1845–1915.

Stay wet and moist, green and juicy.
Hildegard von Bingen
(This was Hildegard's recommendation to the bishops and pope, who were dried up in their thoughts, words, and spirit.)

hours or until the tea is a rich, deep red. This is a cold infusion. The tea will have a refreshing tangy citrus flavor. (I like to sweeten it with maple syrup to taste.) Stir well. Add about $1/4$ cup of rose water or orange flower water to magically enhance the flavor.

Fruit-Syrup Seltzers

In a small saucepan gently heat your favorite berry jam with a little hot water or fruit liqueur, stirring to blend into a syrup. Add this to sparkling water and ice or drizzle over your lover as dessert.

Sensuous Smoothies

Smoothies are a great way to breakfast or pick up energy. Share this ambrosial delight with your sweetie before, during, or after things get you hot and bothered.

Blend a frozen banana with a cup of fresh or frozen berries, peaches, nectarines, and a very ripe persimmon, or mangoes, papayas, and 1 cup of orange juice. Other options might include adding a pinch of cloves, $1/3$ cup yogurt or ice cream, 1 spoonful of protein powder, or a small spoonful of bee pollen. Chocolate or vanilla cordial added to a strawberry or peach smoothie is exquisite, or try Damiana Cordial (page 79) with an orange smoothie.

Luscious Lassi

These frothy beverages, one sweet, one not, make a refreshing time-out when things get a bit hot under the collar. Blend 1 cup of chilled milk and 1 cup of yogurt with 3 teaspoons of honey or sugar. Add a splash of rose water, a pinch of salt, and 1 teaspoon of lemon juice.

Or, to 2 cups of yogurt add 1 peeled and seeded cucumber, a pinch of salt, and a small handful of spearmint. Blend well and chill before serving.

Eugène Agelou, steroscopic photograph (one half shown here), reprinted in 1910.

Chapter 6

Beauty and the Bath:
Lascivious Lavage

I grew up in a pine, cedar, and fir forest on the edge of a beautiful lake in northern California. In the summer we would find wonderful, tiny lavender-colored butterflies that hung out on the very edge of the water in our serene and protected cove. We would pick them up to look at them and then put them down again, using the iridescent sparkles they left on our fingers as eye shadow. Then we would squash berries and use the juice for lipstick. Many a summer after a winter of heavy snows there would be an overabundance of ladybugs everywhere, which would become rubies in our hair. The tiny bright-green tree froggies that appeared after a summer rain would be placed on our white tee shirts as emeralds! As the Lady of the Lake, I would carry a bright-yellow mullein flower stalk as my staff. On warm summer nights we would sneak down to the lake and go skinny-dipping in the moonlight as the rising moon danced its way across the water.

She is a garden enclosed,
my sister, my promised bride;
a garden enclosed,
a sealed fountain.
Your shoots form an orchard of
*   pomegranate trees,*
the rarest essences are yours:
nard and saffron,
calamus and cinnamon,
with all the incense-bearing trees;
myrrh and aloes,
with the subtlest odors.
Fountain that makes the gardens fertile,
well of living water,
streams flowing down from Lebanon.

Song of Sol. 4:12–4:15

A woman touched by the goddess of love,
finds time to dedicate to the care of her own
body, hair, and manner of dress.

It is vitally important for us to take time
out to create a space of peace and tranquillity
in which to nurture ourselves. Then we can pass

Venus Disrobing for the Bath, Lord Frederic
Leighton, 1830–1896.

on some of that tranquillity and peacefulness to others. A walk in the freshness of a forest or barefoot on the beach works wonders. We could also bathe in beautifully scented waters. "Taking the waters" together was almost as important as spirituality to the ancients. Bathing honors the sense of touch and is a tactile aphrodisiac. Some of my favorite scenes are the mosaic-tiled Greek and Roman baths, which were convivial gathering places for the community. Business and pleasure were both conducted in the baths. In the Roman culture men and women shared the marble baths; perhaps the concept of orgies came from this. In harems women would join together to bathe one another and wash and comb each other's hair. Picture yourself there: As the steam rises, you can almost smell the myrrh, sandalwood, jasmine, and orange blossom.

Romantic, Seductive Aromas to Inspire Juiciness

Because scents are significant memory-triggers and turn-ons, we are all able to associate certain scents with memorable events. The aromas of gardenias floating in a bowl of water; pink jasmine on a warm evening; warm, spicy, earthy patchouli; ancient, sensuous sandalwood; woodsy cedar; smooth, erotic amber; mouthwatering musk; tropical, sexy ylang ylang; spring lilacs; and the scent of pumpkin pies and spicy cinnamon rolls baking can certainly be a turn-on. We know what favorite fragrances do for us. Use a drop or two of essential oils on the pillowcase, in the bath, or behind the ear to remind you of your erotic self. When sniffing aromas on the skin, whether yours or another's, first inhale slowly through the nostrils. Without moving to another place, exhale through the nostrils over the fragrance. This warms the skin and the scent. Inhale again, slowly. *Aaahhhh!* Dessert for the brain.

I have asked different people all across the country what fragrance or aroma gets them in the mood. Time after time people remembered and associated sexy scents with the first times they felt sexual. For many of them, this was when they were teenagers. For some women it was the scent of Brut aftershave and a warm leather jacket. Some men remember their earliest lovers wearing Chanel No. 5, so whenever they catch this on the breeze, it touches a place

lake where I grew up and starting a bonfire after the first rain. We burned logs of pine and cedar and that sensual, woodsy fragrance would cling to our hair and clothing for days afterward reminding me of some pretty juicy times by the lake! Byzantine women used to burn resins such as frankincense and myrrh with sandalwood on charcoal, then fluff their long robes and hair over the smoke to scent their clothing and body. The purifying aspect of these fragrances would uplift them spiritually, as well.

I have always loved the scent of patchouli. I find myself sniffing someone out in a crowd to catch a secret, extra deep breath. I notice my mouth watering and my face grinning, among other reactions.

Sensuous Love Bath

Bathing alone is luscious. Bathing with a partner can be very sensually arousing. Accoutrements you may wish to include are candlelight, soft music, a fragrant tub, fresh flowers placed around the tub, a sea sponge or loofa, a fluffy towel, a glass of something refreshing and rehydrating, and maybe chocolate.

in the brain that remembers and says, "Yes!" One person commented on how he remembered smooching in the back alley behind a restaurant with its exhaust fan blowing out a delicious barbecue smell to complement the taste of wine on the lips of his lover. Different scents do it for different folks. I remember all of us local teens getting together at the edge of the

To inspire thoughts of a mermaid's haven,

drape a turquoise fishnet over the tub or shower area with seashells, starfish, sand dollars, a sea horse, a sea sponge, and glass baubles intertwined with a bit of lacy moss. Small seashell lights in the bathroom add a nice touch and a candle burning in a seashell can be quite a seductive lure.

Bath Herbs

Taking an herbal bath is like steeping yourself in a giant cup of tea.
Rosemary Gladstar

The bath can be enhanced by floating a flower in the water or by decorating the edges of the tub with shells as an altar to the sea goddess, for whom blues, greens, shells, and seaweeds are sacred.

Place dried or fresh herbs in a handkerchief, cheesecloth, or muslin bag and float this in the tub. Another way to make an herbal bath is to prepare tea in a large canning pot by boiling water and adding about 3 handfuls of dried or 4 handfuls of fresh flowers and herbs. Let this steep, covered, for 20 minutes, then strain into the tub. Your skin is your largest organ. Soaking it will allow your body to absorb the health-giving herbal qualities. So using relaxing herbs such as chamomile, lavender, passionflower, skullcap, and red clover blossoms can be very tranquilizing and peaceful. But don't soak too long if you have a full evening ahead!

One evening I had a quiet house to myself, so I thought I would give myself a special, sensuous bath. I gathered handfuls of fragrant flowers from my garden and floated them in the bathtub. It was beautiful, magical, and rejuvenating. I soaked for about a half hour. When I was ready to get out, I stood up. The beautiful flowers, completely cooked by now, *all* stuck to my wet, relaxed body! I was picking off pieces and petals—what a mess! Then I realized I had pulled the drainplug; now the tub was clogged. So I ran down the hall to the shower to rinse off the melting herbs and flowers. Oops! I clogged that drain, too. I ended up outside in the cold night, hosing myself off in the backyard. I had to laugh at myself. The moral of the story: Don't put a bouquet of loose flowers and herbs in your tub unless you are bored and have nothing to do but pick disintegrating flowers out of your hair and drain. (Or, try using a kitchen sieve or goldfish net to lift the petals out *before* standing up and *before* draining the tub, if you're really passionate for the experience.)

Byzantine Bath Salts

Bathing in sea salts has been favored since antiquity. It adds precious trace minerals from the sea to your bath and creates an oceanic atmosphere for your body.

Remember to inspire sensuality when bathing. Don't soak too long, as it can be overly relaxing—you'll be more interested in finding your pillow than your partner! Soak for 15–20 minutes, tops, which should be relaxing, yet sensual. Place the sea salt in a glass bowl and mix in the oils with a wire whisk, then add essential oils or fragrance oils. If your muscles are extra tense, you can add a scoop of Epsom salts. (Take care with the Epsom salts; they can be too relaxing to be sensual!) If you have very hard water add a scoop of Borax (yes, 20-mule-team borax) to soften the water and your skin. Refined borax has been recommended as an aphrodisiac bath

Sir Lawrence Alma-Tadema, *The Baths of Caracalla*, 1899. Oil on canvas. Private collection.

since the old days, since it is believed to open the blood vessels and help with circulation. This could help to get one in the mood and move the blood to where it is most needed. Proportions are not too important with the salts; equal parts are fine. Rock salt is beautiful in a jar with a little color added to it. The only problem is that you will want the salts to dissolve before sitting in the tub. Otherwise it can feel like little sharp gravel stuck to your bottom! I would recommend using about 1 teaspoon of essential oils to 3 cups of salts. You will want the salts to be strongly scented, since you will only be adding about $^1/_2$ cup of them to your bath *just* before you step in. If you add the salts earlier, as the water is filling the tub, you will miss out on the precious aroma they offer—most of the fragrance will end up on the ceiling of your bathroom. Bathing salts

may be personalized to your mood; they also make a great gift. Store the salts in a jar with a nonmetal lid; the widemouthed glass jars with latch-down lids are perfect. You can use a seashell as a scoop. Do *not* use mint, cinnamon, or thyme essential oils in the bath, as they are very strong and can burn the skin. Go lightly with all oils until you get to know their strengths in the bath.

Lavender and rose geranium essential oils (about 1 teaspoon each to 3 cups of salts) are good for balancing and soothing, yet are gently uplifting. They can provide a tranquil and very harmonizing effect in situations of tension and conflict.

If the true essences of other oils like rose, jasmine, neroli (orange flower oil), or amber are what you desire in your bath, try anointing your body with one of these precious oils before climbing into the tub. This way, expensive and valuable oils will not go down the drain. As you steep yourself in the hot tub, notice the fragrance rising. Inhale slowly and deeply. Rose is excellent for opening the heart as well as for helping to heal a broken heart. Jasmine is reminiscent of a warm sensuous summer's eve. Try adding vanilla extract directly into the bath as you step in.

Diana's Delight

To 3 cups of salts add:
  1 teaspoon ylang ylang
    essential oil
  1 teaspoon orange oil
  $^1/_4$ teaspoon clove oil
  1–5 drops patchouli

Bubble Bath

Bathing in bubbles has always been a magical and sensuous experience for me. As a kid I loved to pile the soap bubbles on certain places and run naked through the house until they all blew away—while I was looking for a towel.

Making your own scented bubble bath is very easy. Start with an unscented liquid soap such as Lifetree home soap, which is biodegradable. Use 1/2 cup liquid soap mixed with 1/2 cup distilled water or rose water. Then add 1/2–1 teaspoon essential oil or fragrance oil. Shake well and squirt it into the tub! This makes a great liquid soap for the shower or even the kitchen sink. What a way to start the day in your erotic kitchen! A combination of vanilla and musk, vanilla and orange, patchouli and orange, or gardenia, lily of the valley, or coconut can inspire a whole day or evening.

Milk Bath

Canned coconut milk added to the tub is softening and very moisturizing for the skin. The milk disperses and the coconut oil floats. Massage the oil into your skin as you stand up.

Instant powdered milk can be poured into the tub along with your favorite fragrance: 1 cup instant milk powder to 1/2 teaspoon essential oil. Cleopatra was said to have bathed in fresh ass's milk. Fresh cream has a higher fat content than milk and is extra moisturizing. Fresh cream and rose water together can create a rich tub of rose cream in which to luxuriate. Anoint yourself with attar of roses before stepping in.

Bodacious Body, Bath, and Massage Oil

Whole-body massage can be seen as an exquisite art form and a significant part of both foreplay and afterplay.

There are several oils that may be used, since various vegetable oils provide different sensations for the skin. Almond and sesame oils are in the middle, halfway between light and heavy. Coconut, canola, and grapeseed oils are at the very light end of the spectrum, while olive oil, cocoa butter, and jojoba oil are heavier. Hemp seed oil is very heavy. Be sure to sniff oils before purchasing, if possible. Grapeseed oil, for instance, can become rancid easily. I love

a light olive oil for full body massage. Ghee is great for erotic massage—you don't need to keep adding as much oil to the body as you do with lighter oils.

Mix 1 cup of almond, olive, or sesame oil with $1/2$ teaspoon of essential oils or fragrance oils in a plastic squirt bottle. Shake well. This is ready to use for a massage, or you can add 1–2 teaspoons per bath just before you step in. Or use as a rich moisturizing oil after bathing, while the skin is still damp. A little squirt will do you. You can personalize the fragrances; they make great gifts, as well.

Cocoa Butter

Try rubbing your warm body or someone else's warm body with a chunk of cocoa butter as a sensuous moisturizer and/or massage butter. Cocoa butter is the oily part of the cocoa bean and has an exquisite chocolaty fragrance. (It does not taste like chocolate, however.) This botanical butter is one of the finest moisturizers for the skin. It is used to prevent and soothe windburn and is massaged on pregnant bellies to prevent stretch marks. Its chocolate scent helps overcome morning sickness, too! Cocoa butter makes a tempting, personal, erotic massage butter, and a small piece of it inserted into the vagina melts quickly and helps with vaginal lubrication. *Caution:* Cocoa butter is not latex-friendly.

As a teenager growing up on a lake in the summers, I spent a lot of time sunbathing in the pure mountain air. One day I ran out of tanning oil and decided to use a little cocoa butter instead. I buttered myself up and fell asleep in the hammock in the sun. I awoke to a very strange tickly sensation. A whole litter of seven kittens was sitting on me, licking the butter off! It was wonderful and titillating, a good example of a tactile aphrodisiac!

Ghee

Ghee is clarified butter. To make it, melt unsalted butter at a low temperature. When the milk solids settle, skim off the frothy foam floating on top. What is left is a clarified oil excellent for cooking or rubbing on your body. It

never needs refrigeration and does not disturb those who are lactose-intolerant. In India it is rubbed into the skin for nourishment. This clarified butter makes an excellent cream for an erotic massage. A little bit can go a long way.

For an edible "love butter" massage balm, mix a small amount of ghee with a drop of essential oil—orange, rose, anise, bergamot, or vanilla. A few drops of vegetable glycerin or glycerin-based flavorings (found at your natural foods store) may be added to sweeten the balm. Keep in mind that

British postcard, three-color half-tone, post-1902.

ghee, vegetable oils, and essential oils are not la-tex-friendly! Glycerin is a sugar and may antago-nize the good, friendly vaginal bacteria, so leave out the glycerin if you have a yeast condition. The sweetened ghee is quite tantalizing for the rest of the body, however.

Mystic Mists and Sensuous Spritzers

This is an enticing way to put some of your fa-vorite bottles of essential or fragrance oils to use. The mists may be spritzed around a room to lift the spirits, change the mood, refresh and renew, and definitely inspire sensuality. To make a stron-ger perfume fragrance, add more essential oil. For an afterbath or lovemaking spritzer sprayed directly on the skin, make the spray more dilute. Take a sniff of the scents you would like to use. If they are delicate, you may want to add a few more drops. If you take off the cap and swoon, if your eyes water and your ears tingle, use a very small amount in the spray.

In a 4-ounce spray bottle, add 1 teaspoon of vodka to 10–30 drops of essential oil and shake well. Add ¹/₂ cup distilled water and shake well again. Spritz on clothes, bed, hair, curtains, light bulbs, towels. . . .

The vodka is used to help disperse the es-sential oils but the sprays can be made without it. Make sure to use distilled water, as bacteria will grow in tap water.

I encourage you to explore herb shops. Open the little bottles of essential oils and fra-grances and sniff! There will be certain ones, your fragrances, that speak only to you. You can add them to favorite lotions or put a dab on your clothes, on your pillow, or in your car. Patchouli has been a favorite of mine for twenty-five years, and gets spritzed in my closet every so often. I tend to not notice it much, but when I'm out and about, people comment. To my surprise, most people love it. Its scent changes slightly with each person, and as your body warms up it releases its potency. My mom never quite took a liking to it. She thought I was trying to "cover something up." I said no, but that's a great idea! I use it as an underarm deodorant, in my shampoo, and sprayed on my coat. Fragrance is a wonderful way to evoke memories—just experiment, remember, and enjoy yourself.

Some favorite combinations worthy of self-indulgent aromatic exploration:

- Orange/cedarwood
- Patchouli/ylang ylang/clove
- Sandalwood/vanilla
- Orange/anise
- Rose geranium/lavender/orange
- Cedarwood/lemongrass
- Rose water/vanilla extract

After being incredibly popular for thousands of years, sandalwood is now limited for export from India, as most of the trees have either been cut for use in perfumery and incense or burned by fires. If you still have some or are able to find a small bottle, savor it and use it sparingly—a little goes a long way.

The most powerful scent of love, though, is the body's own natural odor. In our society we tend to mask our natural scent synthetically. Spray this here, douche with that there, rinse this out with that. Yet there are very good all-natural deodorants that complement our natural body essences. The essential oils in aromatic plants can enhance our own scents. Even in the plant world fragrance emanates from the reproductive parts of the flower. Try rubbing a small amount of amber fragrance into the armpit area. The warmth of the body releases the scent. Here is an antique aphrodisiac technique that may have its place in modern-day romanticism: A woman would seal a love letter to her beloved with her own yoni essence to remind her lover what was waiting upon his return home! Men and women may use their own love juices as the ultimate cologne.

In the springtime the rounded hips of amorous women are adorned with silken garments colored with saffron. Languid with passion, they rub sandalwood paste mixed with sweet flowers, saffron and musk on their breasts.

Ritusamhara

Chapter 7

Sensual Body Work

Yoni

Blessed be thy womb, without which we would not be.

From a Wiccan incantation

Yoni, from the Sanskrit for womb, origin, and source, refers to the vulva and vagina. The term *yoni* stems from a time and place where women were honored as an embodiment of the goddess, as divine feminine energy. Women's genitals should be worshiped and regarded as the sacred symbol of the goddess. The yoni is the divine portal to our sacred inner temple. Each woman's precious flower is as unique as the woman herself. How we feel about our yoni petals and our breasts affects us sexually, emotionally, and physically. We are taught at an early age not to touch ourselves or talk about things relating to our genitals. Yet they are very sacred parts of us, to be respected, honored, pleasured,

---

Vincent Dame (1946–1995), *Plums,* glazed ceramics. Galerie Vignet, Amsterdam. Photograph by Vincent Dame.

and pampered. Yonis come in many different shapes, colors, and sizes; each one is unique, the way our faces are. With a sex-positive attitude, we can open to the beauty that is present in our own bodies. Anaïs Nin called the yoni "the delta of Venus." Also known as the mound of Venus or the triangle of Aphrodite, the yoni is that which connects heaven with earth. When a

Every fruit has its secret.
D. H. Lawrence

woman's yoni is entered by her lover, it should be thought of as a sacred temple, entered slowly, with awareness and sensitivity.

We are all too familiar with the slang terms for yoni. It is interesting to note the different names that were used to refer to our yonis when we were children. Here are some names throughout different cultures that honor the

yoni: chalice, concha, cunnus, doorway of life, fig, flower, fruitful vine, garden gate, gate of jewels, golden gate, grotto, happy valley, heavenly gate, home sweet home, honey pot, inner heart, ivory gate, jade gate, kunti, living fountain, lotus of her wisdom, mysterious gate, mystic rose, sweet papaya, pleasure garden, precious crucible, secret cavern, vulva.

> Your lips, *my promised one,*
> distill wild honey.
> *Honey and milk*
> *are under your tongue;*
> *and the scent of your garments*
> *is like the scent of Lebanon.*
>
> Song of Sol. 4:11

The yoni was once regarded by some cultures as a magical instrument with protective and healing energies. Women in ancient times would expose their yonis as a way to dispel evil and to quiet dangerous storms. When I was about seven, my little friend from next door raced over to tell me that our tree fort had been wrecked by the creepy brothers who shared a fence with us. They had thrown doggy doo-doo all over, and she was livid! As we were examining the mess, two of the brothers stuck their heads over the fence and laughed at us. She immediately pulled down her panties and spread her yoni lips apart with her hands, stuck out her tongue, and made a scary face. They freaked out, ran away, and never bothered us again. She seemed to be in touch with an ancient wisdom used long ago.

Yoni Health and Vaginal Dryness

When your mouth and lips get dry, you put on lip balm or get a sip of water. But what about your lower lips? When you get out of the shower or bathtub, you probably moisturize your skin with lotions and your hair with conditioner. Don't forget to moisturize your lower lips, too! Cleopatra would have used precious oils of olive or sesame. We can also use a small amount of almond or olive oil, cocoa butter, or coconut oil to moisturize these petals and act as an intimate erotic lubricant. (Once again, remember that all vegetable and essential oils are *not* latex-friendly.) While these vegetable oils do provide a sensual, moisturizing lubricant, they should not take the place of foreplay. Natural lubrication occurs when a woman is caressed and stimulated.

For an herbal experience in oral pleasuring, try sucking on a strong peppermint candy before engaging in oral sex.

Yoni Lip Balm or Lingam Love Butter

> ¹/₄ cup almond oil
> 2 tablespoons grated cocoa butter, packed to measure
> 1–2 tablespoons grated beeswax
> 2 vitamin E capsules
> Fragrance, optional

Gently melt ingredients over low heat. Remove from heat and let cool. (If the butter is too soft, melt it again and add a little more beeswax. If the butter is too hard, melt it and add a little more almond oil.) When the mixture has cooled, stir in 2 vitamin E capsules, and fragrance if desired. (One-fourth teaspoon of ylang ylang or lavender oil may be added. Equal parts of anise and orange oils—¹/₄ teaspoon each—are delectable.) This mixture can be used as a massage balm, moisturizer, and great personal lubricant. (*Caution:* This is *not* latex-friendly.)

For a tasty edible massage balm, you can whisk ¹/₂ teaspoon of nonalcoholic, glycerin-based flavor extracts (found in natural food stores) into the above recipe as it is cooling. Try

The Blue Veil, photograph, late nineteenth century.

vanilla, orange, coconut, strawberry, mint, or a combination.

Rich Red Oil

3 tablespoons dried or crushed alkanet root
1 cup almond oil

For a beautiful, naturally red-colored oil steep 3 tablespoons of alkanet root in 1 cup of almond oil for a couple of days. Shake daily, then strain through a cheesecloth or strainer. This natural dye gives out its color in oil only, not in water. It can be used in the Yoni Lip Balm.

Chocolate Lip Balm

$^1/_2$ cup grated cocoa butter
2 tablespoons coconut oil
1 tablespoon grated chocolate
1 vitamin E capsule, optional
1 teaspoon vanilla extract, optional
$^1/_2$ teaspoon honey, optional

Gently heat the grated cocoa butter, coconut oil, and grated chocolate over hot water, stirring well. As this cools, a capsule of vitamin E, 1 teaspoon of vanilla extract, and $^1/_2$ teaspoon of honey may be whisked in if desired.

When women complain of vaginal dryness, I have a checklist to go through that may be helpful.

First, it is important to drink plenty of water—two quarts daily is recommended. One quart may be of tonic herbal teas.

Second, doing kegel exercises daily helps improve circulation to the yoni and brings our attention to this area. Kegels are so valuable that it is never really too soon to practice them. I remember reading about the "love muscle sexercises" in a women's magazine my aunt left lying around the house when I was fourteen. It described just how to get in contact with the muscle used in this exercise. Next time you pee, try to stop the flow of urine. That is the muscle to squeeze and release. You can squeeze and release the muscle slowly, and then a few times more quickly. When you are in the line at the post office or grocery store, why not squeeze and release? While others are complaining about the long lines, you will be grinning away. If you see other women grinning quietly, you'll know what they are up to! To help you remember to do the exercises, put a rose sticker up on your bathroom mirror to remind you to squeeze and release while brushing your teeth. Maybe you'll brush longer and have fewer dental problems! Also, waiting for the red light to turn green with the car radio on, you can squeeze and release to rock and roll, jazz, or the Gypsy Kings!

This exercise helps us to hold the pelvic floor and organs such as the uterus, ovaries, and intestines in place so that, as we age, we don't leak urine when we cough, sneeze, or laugh and end up having to wear diapers. But the best result from doing this exercise regularly is the effect it has on sex life and orgasms! Orgasms become stronger, deeper, and more ecstatic; your partner will feel the difference during lovemaking.

You can start with 10 squeezes and work up to 30, then up to 100, a couple of times a day. If you have a job where you sit most of the time, it is important to change positions regularly so the energy doesn't stagnate in the lower abdomen. Walk around and do a few squats regularly to help the lymph system keep moving.

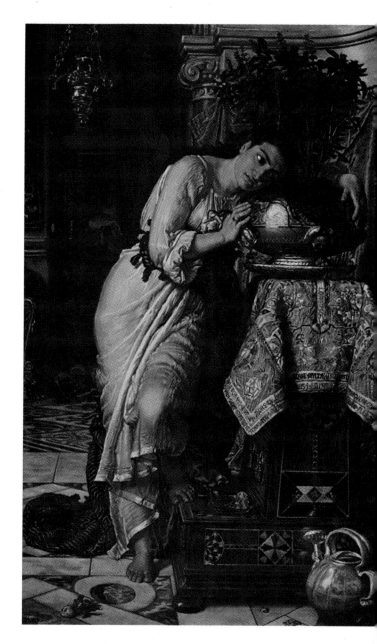

William Holman Hunt, *Isabella and the Pot of Basil*, 1867. Delaware Art Museum.

Okay, on to the *third* thing to check if you are experiencing vaginal dryness. Diet and hormonal changes can affect juiciness. A diet rich in phytoestrogens, which means a plant-based diet with lots of greens such as kale, collards, mustard greens, dandelion greens, and escarole and foods such as tofu or soy milk that help nourish you and fill your own estrogen-receptor sites. Fennel, black cohosh, and *Vitex* berries regulate and normalize your hormones, as do vitamin E and the other vitamins and herbs mentioned earlier. Antihistamines will dry up your snuffy nose as well as your vaginal secretions. There are other prescription drugs that may also dry the yoni. Cocoa butter inserted vaginally will help with lubrication. If you are feeling unusually dry, check with your physician about adjusting or changing your prescription. Some prescription drugs also take away the libido, so consult your doctor about this.

The *fourth* thing to consider are aspects of clothing, douching, and tampons. It is important to allow air to caress this very treasured part of our bodies. Our clothing can affect the health of our yonis. Yonis love natural fabrics like silk and cotton as opposed to synthetic fabrics that do not allow the area to breathe. If you wear pantyhose under your pants and wear underwear underneath everything, there is a good chance of yeast infections and oxygen deprivation. I joke in workshops about wearing pantyhose over your head and face and trying to breath all day. Free your petals by going without underwear some of the time or all of the time. Your yoni will love it. Let her be warmed in the sun for a few minutes or maybe give her a moonbath. If you are wearing a dress try a pair of silk boxers, which can double as a slip. They also let air circulate and feel incredibly sexy against your body. Wearing pants that are too tight may cause trouble in the nether region. This seemed to be more of a problem in the 1970s.

It is fine to wash with plain water sometimes, as washing your yoni with hard bar soaps can be too drying. For soap to be held in a bar shape, it must be very alkaline, which can be too drying for delicate parts. A liquid soap can be more gentle. Watch for perfumes, since they can irritate. Splashing on good, plain old water can refresh you and allow your bodily juices to cleanse your yoni naturally. When we are turned on, our body naturally lubricates and cleanses itself. Douching washes away our natural secretions and dries out the delicate tissues. We don't need to smell like fake spring flowers or artificial strawberries down there. In cultures where the yoni and women are honored as embodiments of the goddess, their bodies are anointed with their own inner juices as a blessing and the best aphrodisiac.

Would you put a tampon in your mouth and suck on it? No, of course not! Would you stick one up your nose when it gets drippy? Probably not. Ahh, then why do we plug up and block our life's blood, our creative juices? So we can look smooth in those tight white jeans? That was the advertising for tampons when I was a teen. Some tampons are made from dioxin-bleached cotton and synthetic fibers dipped in chemicals that can make you bleed more, so that you use more tampons. They dry out vaginal tissues and can cause mild to severe itching, irritation, and unjuiciness. The message women get about this powerful time of month is to pretend we're not really bleeding and to stuff ourselves in our clothes so we don't look bloated. Block the flow. Could this be blocking the creative flow in our lives? How do you feel about your body during this time? Negative feelings about our bodies can affect us sexually. What was it like for you during your first bleeding time, or moontime? We cycle with the moon. We become full, like the moon, once a month. During this time we may feel more like going within and not being out there in the world so much. There was a time when women were honored during their moontimes. In the villages they would go to a special hut where they would be given hot teas and broth, and while they were bleeding, their families were looked after by women who were not bleeding. They honored their dreams during this time also. Well, we have come a long way since then, but if we honor our natural cycles as we bleed and when we ovulate, there will be times during the month when we can feel a stronger sex drive. Some women feel most passionate during ovulation, some just after bleeding, and some during bleeding. These are all normal and change according to the seasons and planetary influences, as do our hormones and relationships. Maybe it is time for us to make friends with our bodies. Menstrual lingerie could be made in the form of velvety-soft flannel. Reusable, washable cotton pads are an excellent alternative to the synthetic menstrual pads sold commercially for external use.

Natural sea sponges cut to fit as menstrual protection may provide an alternative to tampons. Natural food stores now carry an oxygen-bleached-cotton natural tampon. If you need to wear these, be careful not to leave them in for more than an hour at a time so that what is meant to flow out of the body is not reabsorbed into the system.

Fifth, think juicy thoughts. Think about sexual imagery. What turns you on? Can you share what turns you on with your lover? Also, are you receiving enough caressing and stimulation to become lubricated naturally? This can take time, but is *so* worth doing slowly.

Lingams and Prostate Health

Lingam is the sacred Sanskrit term for a man's organ of pleasure and regeneration. In India stone lingam statues are everywhere; fruit, flowers, and rice are left as offerings to them. Some of the names given to honor the lingam are arrow of love, diamond scepter, *il santo membro,* jade flute, jade scepter, key of desire, magic wand, *membrum virile,* mushroom of immortality, phallus, plough, rod, spear, and wand of desire, to mention a few.

Self-pleasuring massage with focus on the perineum and kegel exercises are two of the best things men can do regularly to maintain and protect prostate health. The same squeeze-and-release technique described above for women is also very important for men to do. It helps to tone the pelvic muscles and internally massages the prostate gland. Regular self-pleasuring and orgasm can help prostate energy from stagnating due to lack of stimulation. Keep it functioning. So gentlemen, to massage your perineum, start with a nice lotion and massage the area between the anus and the testicles, stroking with your fingers in a circular motion. While it may seem more fun to have your lover do this, be sure to take the time to do this special massage for yourself, as well.

Pumpkin seeds are rich in zinc; taken regularly, they are a tonic for the prostate. Oatmeal and green-oat tea, tablets, or tincture can help you to "feel your oats" again. Saw palmetto berries as a tincture or liqueur nourish, strengthen, and tone the prostate gland and surrounding tissues and may be both used as a preventive

Shiva lingam garlanded with offering flowers and substances, Bengal. Photograph by Nik Douglas.

for infection and taken during an infection for relief. Men can also learn to orgasm without ejaculating to help retain their precious body fluids, rich in lecithin, minerals, and protein. There are books, tapes, and videos available for learning useful techniques.

Impotence

Something that can affect men of any age at one time or another is impotence, or the inability to achieve or sustain erection. This can be caused by physical debility or exhaustion, anxiety, older age, overindulgence, or sexually toxic drugs. A nourishing, balanced diet that includes herbal tonics, physical exercise, and an adjustment in mental attitude can work wonders. The use of tantric sexual techniques, hatha yoga, and creative meditation, as well as a change in lifestyle can also be very helpful. A trip to your local adult toy store can prove to be quite "uplifting." Many couples are exploring their sexuality in a new light. Adult toys, erotic picture books and literature, and role-playing with emphasis on sensual attire can bring a delicious new flavor to your relationship.

Impotence may also be brought on by drugs used to treat high blood pressure or other problems. Discuss this with your physician to find out about alternatives. Ginseng root, green oats, and cannabis can dispel impotence if used correctly. Psychoactive substances, ceremonies, and magical invocations may be options, as well. In tantric practice, the encumbrance of performance is replaced by a fresh perspective on sexuality, with a focus on mutual enrichment.

Breast Health

With the outrageous incidence of breast cancer in our culture today, it is important to edu-

Right: From an erotic postcard.
Opposite: French postcard, tinted photograph, post-1908.

cate ourselves about diet and lifestyle and to recognize how our attitudes about our bodies affect our breasts. I encourage all women to make friends with their breasts now. You may start by lovingly massaging your breasts in front of a mirror, maybe with a little rose geranium essential oil added to almond oil or your favorite lotion. First warm your hands by rubbing them together. Then, starting at the center of the breasts, spiral out, then spiral in. Try between 20 and 30 rotations each day. Love your breasts! (You can talk to them; they may even tell you what foods to eat or not eat for them!) Red clover blossom tea and cleavers tea are cleansing, tonic, and health-promoting for the breasts, as is vitamin E taken regularly. A great blessing to say while massaging or anointing the breasts is: *Bless my breasts, formed in strength and beauty, which give and receive nourishment and pleasure.*

Belly Dancing for Health

Once, during an evening performance, a beautiful dancer of long ago in Egypt generously poured rose water into a small goblet, which she then held in her teeth as she danced, undulating across the floor

without spilling a drop. She lasciviously shimmied her loins as her writhing snake arms and enchanting eyes captivated a male guest. On her toes, with the glass still in her teeth, she encircled his waist with her arms, tilting her head back, letting the

MmE MATA HARI «Danse Indienne»

rose water trickle down his face. As the glass fell to the floor, she paused and kissed his lips and was off … with twirls and shimmies, breathlessly into her finale.

This ancient dance was originally performed by women for women, especially for women in labor to help the process of nature. The dance strengthens, tones, and massages the digestive organs, while aiding circulation to the reproductive organs, tissues, and ligaments. Its undulating movements are similar to a snake's coiling and uncoiling. Men can also be great belly dancers. The dance's isolation movements tone the abdominal muscles and are great fun to practice. Many of these sensuous motions may be used during lovemaking.

After stretching, when your body feels warmed up, put on some lively, upbeat dancing music for 20 or 30 minutes. Shake and shimmy, rotating your hips, dance for yourself. Make up new moves—don't worry, no one is watching. Dance out your stress, your emotions; dance for

Gaston Saintpierre, detail from *Women's Wedding Party in Algeria*, 1870s. Oil painting. Private collection.

fun. Dancing feeds the spirit and tones the body.

Jwala, a beautiful tantrika, taught me a pelvic–rock exercise that is very helpful in loosening up and bringing awareness to the pelvic area. This exercise can be done by both men and women. Lie on your back with your knees bent and your arms relaxed at your sides. Inhale as you tilt your pelvis down, which allows your lower back to arch up. As you exhale, rock your pelvis upward so that your lower back touches the floor. Allow a wavelike, undulating movement to roll all the way up through your neck. Let your legs and knees open and close naturally. Start with about 30 repetitions the first day and slowly add repetitions as you build control and stamina.

Try rolling your belly. First relax your stomach muscles, then suck in only the top portion of your belly, then release. Then suck in the lower portion of your belly, then release. Getting in touch with this part of your body may be new to you. Practice in front of a mirror a little each day, learning to isolate certain muscles. As you hold the upper part of your belly in, the lower part will be relaxed. Practice making eyes at yourself in the mirror. Roll your shoulders back, lift your chest up, then lower it back down. Making small circles with the hips to some favorite music wakes up the pelvic area. Dance seductively to any favorite music that inspires you. Dress in a long, flowing robe and tie scarves around your head and waist. Pin a necklace on your headscarf. You may enjoy enrolling in a belly-dance class.

Mirror Magic: Making Friends with Your Body

Sit or stand naked in front of the mirror. Put a little oil or lotion in your palm and rub vigorously to warm it up, then massage your belly in a clockwise circle to relax the area and help the energy to flow freely. Rub your hands vigorously again and place them over your back and kidney area. This helps circulation and warmth go to the root chakra, the source of our sexual energy.

Then lovingly massage your yoni or lingam. (When was the last time you really looked at your beautiful genitals in the mirror?) Women, notice how unique your precious petals are! So flowerlike! Anoint your inner thighs with a favorite fragrant oil. Taking on a positive attitude toward sex can begin the healing process for many reproductive imbalances. A beautifully magic massage oil may be made by adding up to 5 drops attar of rose oil to 1 ounce of almond oil. Shake well and massage it into your inner thighs from the knees up to the genital area, making sure to include the lower abdomen. This oil massaged over the heart helps to make the special connection between heart and genitals. Rose is helpful in working with sexual-abuse issues.

Deep Breathing

Breath is life! By breathing deeply we are breathing in life. Your breath is your connection with the divine. Deep breathing revitalizes, rebalances, and cleanses your entire body. We tend to forget to breathe deeply into the belly instead of shallowly into the chest. Start to notice *when* and *if* you hold your breath. Sometimes it seems the air gets stuck in the solar plexus. Massage the area from between the breasts down toward the belly button to loosen up any knots. This will help the blood to flow properly to the lower part of the body, reproductive organs included. If there is pain or tension in a particular area, breathe into that part of the body and allow the tension to leave as you exhale.

My son was born at home. I remember seeing his new body, freshly born, before his first breath. He was a strange bluish-purple. We all seemed to be holding our breath, waiting for him to breathe. Then one of the midwives reminded us all to breathe, and when we did, he did. He started to pink up from his heart area outward until a beautiful shade of baby rose-pink came over him. He breathed life in.

Visualize your breath filling your abdomen with beautiful light (you can envision colors like spring green or rose pink). Breathe in slowly through your nose and hold it while squeezing the kegel muscle, then exhale through your mouth as you release the muscle.

Breathe into your center. For women the center is the uterus. For men, the center is the prostate gland. Breathe from this area, giving it permission to light up. Even if an organ has been surgically removed, the body holds the memory of that organ. Breathe in light and see it glowing like a bright sun shining. When we are feeling centered we are able to walk in balance with nature and with our own natures.

If you are needing to be grounded and centered, pretend you are a tree and give your roots permission to burrow deep into the earth to root you firmly. Your spine is the tree trunk; let it light up. Breathe in the light. Hug a tree. Make friends with a special tree you can go to and sit with your spine against its trunk. Talk or sing to the tree. Trees are our ancestors.

Chapter 8

Ancient Aphrodisiacs

Some of the "olde thyme" aphrodisiac recipes that have been popular over the ages are bird's nest soup (composed of seaweed held together with the bird's saliva and the spawn of small fish), animal genitalia, lizard paté, dove brains, skink tails, shark fins, powdered deer antlers, sow secretions, cow vulvae, dried black ants in olive oil, sperm whale intestinal secretions, rhinoceros horns, tiger whiskers, and the melted fat from the hump of a camel (used as an external genital lubricant)—just to mention a few.

The most unimaginable ingredients have been used for centuries. In *The Kama Sutra,* for example, one instruction is to "boil a testicle of a ram or goat in milk, add sugar and drink!" (I wonder, should this be pureed and blended like a smoothie? Or does it float around like an ice cube?) In the Middle Ages one popular aphrodisiac required taking 3 pubic hairs and 3 hairs from the left armpit. The hairs would then be burned on a hot shovel and pulverized. The resulting powder was inserted into a piece of bread, and the bread dipped in soup and fed to a lover for faithfulness.

A more tantalizing aphrodisiac than stolen body hairs, for most palates anyway, might be the tomato. Tomatoes are believed to have originated in Peru. They were introduced to Europe by the Spaniards in the sixteenth century. Because tomatoes were thought to stimulate sexuality, they were called "love apples" in Europe.

Another fruit, the pomegranate is a symbol of fertility and abundance. The Roman encyclopedist Pliny the Elder described this delicious fruit as an aphrodisiac. Pomegranate seeds are mixed with powdered sugar at Oriental weddings and offered to the guests. When the newlyweds enter their new home, pomegranates are broken on the floor, the bursting seeds symbolizing that the marriage will be blessed by many children. Today they are used in fertility magic.

Like body parts and certain foods, precious stones and pearls have long been associated with the power to stimulate sexual desire, not only when presented as gifts, but also when consumed. Pulverized agate is reportedly especially effective. Cleopatra dissolved pearls in vinegar and honey, then sipped this beverage. She was known to have very beautiful skin and hair and, since she managed to have both Julius Caesar and Marc Anthony as lovers, the potion may be considered successful. Precious gemstones were pulverized and painted on the eyes and face as makeup to bring alluring, luminescent qualities to the skin.

Persians used crushed pearls and rubies, gold dust, and ambergris to make pastilles, which they ate as an aphrodisiac. Chaucer, again from a food angle, recommended garlic, onions, leeks, mushrooms, frog's bones, and dried chicken tongues to do the trick. It is said that

Still Life, Magnus Otto Sophus Petersen, 1837–1904.

Primitive Passion Provokers

Hot lavender, mints, savory, marjoram . . .
are given to men of middle age.

Shakespeare, *The Winter's Tale*, 1610

Place a live frog in an anthill and leave until the ants have cleaned the bones; then take the heart-shaped bone and the hook-shaped bone; keep the first yourself but hook the second in the clothing of a loved one.

African American folklore

Burdock seeds in a mortar pounde them. Add of three-yeris-old goat ye lefte testycle and from ye back heris of a whyte whelpe one pynche of poudre, ye heris to be cutte on ye firste daye of ye newe moon and burne on ye seventh daye. Infuse alle ye items in a bottel halfe fylled with brandye. Leve uncorked twenty-one dayes to receive astral influence. Cook on ye twenty-firste daye until ye thicke consistency is reched. Add four droppes of crocodyle semen and passe through fylter. Rubbe mixture on genitalia and await ye result.

From a medieval grimoire

This apple, dear sisters, is a token of everything that arouses lust and sensual delights. Beware.

A Handbook for Nuns, 1200

Cook the ground powder of the chrysanthemum stone with water until a thick paste appears. While cooking, stir in the pulverized wings of butterflies. Dry mixture. Add a few drops of honey and roll mixture into tiny pills. A pill must be secreted into the sleeve of the beloved, who is then rendered submissive to all advance.

Ancient Chinese love philter

Artichokes! Artichokes!
Heats the body and the spirit.
Heats the genitals.

Parisian street vendor's cry

A book of verses, beneath the bough,
A jug of wine, a loaf of bread—
and thou,
Beside me singing in the wilderness—
Oh, wilderness were Paradise enow!

Omar Khayyam,
Rubaiyat, eleventh century

To increase ye powers, take a cock sparrow and pluck it whilst living, then throw it to ten wasps who will sting it to death. Add the intestines of a black raven and oil of lilac plus chamomile. Cook it all in beef fat until the flesh is in shreds. Put into a bottle and hold near for use. Ye shall see marvels.

Lucayos Cookbook, 1660

If thou wilt that a woman bee not vicious nor desire another, take the private members of a woolfe and the haires which doth grow on the cheekes or eyebrowes of him and the haires which bee under his beard, and burne it all and give it to her to drinke, when she knoweth not and she shal desire no other.

Albertus Magnus,
Book of the Marvels of the World,
thirteenth century

Boil an ass's penis together with onions and a large quantity of corn. Feed this dish to fowl, which you eat afterward. This will increase the size and capacity of a man's penis.

Sheikh Nefzawi, *The Perfumed Garden*

in South America some women serve coffee filtered through their well-worn undies to the objects of their desire. And one of the latest substances thought to induce a frenzy of wild passion is green M & Ms!

Historically, nuns were forbidden to eat beans, as they were considered too stimulating to "that" part of the body.

During Roman times, a popular way to treat sexual problems was organotherapy. This therapy is based on the belief that the consumption of a healthy animal organ can cure illnesses in the corresponding human organ. In fact, the Romans ate all kinds of animal genitalia, including penises, vulvae, wombs, and testes from monkeys to cocks to deer. Stuffed womb of pig and cow were eaten to increase fertility.

Spanish Fly *(Cantharis)*

This iridescent green beetle was snuck into unsuspecting lovers' drinks. *It is very dangerous,* causing irreversible damage to the urinary tract or death! Some soldiers in France who ate frog legs noticed that they all had painful erections that would not go away. The frog stomachs were dissected, and many of these green beetles were found in them. The men had been poisoned, but the frogs were unaffected.

Pie of Bulls' Testicles

Take 4 bulls' testicles and boil them in water and salt. Strip the membrane that covers them. Slice, sprinkle with salt, pepper, cinnamon, and nutmeg.

Vulvae Steriles, or Cow Vulvas

This was a favorite libido enhancer of ancient Romans.

Take that part of a cow, clean it well, put it to marinate in white wine in which you have cooked chopped onion, celery, fennel, peppercorns, ginger, saffron, and salt. Marinate a few hours, roll it in flour, then brown it. Add lemon juice before serving.

Resources

Herbal Sources

Avena Botanicals
Box 365
West Rockport, ME 04865
This is a source of exceptional quality products. Avena herbalist Deb Soule grows the herbs used in her products in her lovely herb gardens or wildcrafts them herself. She has a special line of products for women.

Green Terrestrial
P.O. Box 41
Route 9W
Milton, NY 12547
Wise-woman herbalist Pam Montgomery wildcrafts and grows her own plants and makes a wonderful line of medicinal herbal products.

Herbalist and Alchemist
P.O. Box 458
Bloomsbury, NJ 08804
An excellent selection of organic and wildcrafted herbal tinctures.

The Herb Wyfe
17 West Main Street
Wickford, RI 02852
This small shop offers a fine selection of herbs, oils, containers, and other materials needed for making your own herbal products.

Jean's Greens

RR 1 Box 57
Medusa, NY 12120
This small company has a wonderful selection of freshly dried organic and wildcrafted herbs, as well as oils, containers, beeswax, and other materials needed for making herbal products.

Jeanne Rose's Herbal Products

219 Carl Street
San Francisco, CA 94117
Well-known herbalist and author Jeanne Rose makes a wonderful line of natural cosmetics and herbal products.

Mountain Rose Herbs

20818 High St.
North San Juan, CA 95960
Mountain Rose supplies bulk herbs, beeswax, books, oils, and containers.

New England Botanicals

P.O. Box 6
Shelburne Falls, MA 01370
Wise-woman herbalist Gail Ulrich offers an excellent line of herbal tinctures and medicinal products that she makes herself.

Rejuvenessence—Botanica Erotica

P.O. Box 2
Sebastopol, CA 95473
707-824-1365
Co-owned by author Diana De Luca and Dae Williams, Rejuvenessence—Botanica Erotica specializes in all natural sensual face and body care and luscious handmade herbal erotic products. Wholesale or retail catalog available.

Sage Mountain Herb Products

P.O. Box 420
East Barre, VT 05649
This is a small, family-run business that provides exceptional quality tinctures and other herbal products. All products are formulated by Rosemary Gladstar and are made of organically grown and wildcrafted herbs.

Simpler's Botanicals

P.O. Box 39
Forestville, CA 95436
This small business offers a line of exceptional handcrafted herbal and aromatherapy products made by experienced herbalists.

Toys, Advice, and Inspiration

Annie Sprinkle

http://www.heck.com/annie/
sprinkleshow.html

http://www.heck.com/annie/yoni.html (to
check out her yoni massage)

Annie Sprinkle, sacred prostitute/porn star now
sex guru/performance artist, is a wealth of inspiration and pleasure! Check out her guide-
lines for an ecstatic yoni massage.

Blowfish

http://www.blowfish.com

Good products for great sex! The Blowfish
website is for people to browse and enjoy sex-
positive products and information. They cater
to all genders, persuasions, orientations, and
varieties of relationships.

E-Sensuals

P.O. Box 1818
Sebastopol, CA 95472
1-800-9-TANTRA (1-800-982-6872)
707-823-3063 Fax: 707-829-9542
e-mail: catalog@tantra.com
http://tantra.com
The E-Sensuals catalog offers educational ma-
terial related to tantra and sacred sexuality.

Good Vibrations

1210 Valencia Street
San Francisco, CA 94110
415-974-8980
1-800-289-8423 (1-800-BUY-VIBE)
http://www.goodvibes.com

When you visit this online store you can shop
for sex toys, erotica, and adult videos, tour an
antique vibrator museum, and read the latest
sex information and news. Good Vibrations
believes that sexual pleasure is everyone's birth-
right, and that access to sexual materials and
accurate sex information promotes health and
happiness. It is a worker-owned cooperative
with two retail stores, a publishing company
called Down There Press, and two catalogs,
Good Vibrations and *The Sexuality Library*.

Libido

http://www.indra.com/libido
Libido is a publication designed for enlightened
adults, featuring the best American erotica,
short fiction, photography, poetry, humor, news,
reviews, and surprises.

Bibliography and Recommended Reading

Ackerman, Diane. *A Natural History of Love.* New York: Random House, 1994.

———. *A Natural History of the Senses.* New York: Random House, 1990.

Ash, Russell. *Sir Lawrence Alma-Tadema.* New York: Harry N. Abrams, Inc., 1990.

Austen, Hallie Iglehart. *The Heart of the Goddess: Art, Myth, and Meditations of the World's Sacred Feminine.* Berkeley, Calif.: Wingbow Press, 1990.

Buonaventura, Wendy. *Serpent of the Nile: Women and Dance in the Arab World.* London: Saqi Books, 1989.

Camphausen, Rufus C. *The Encyclopedia of Erotic Wisdom: A Reference Guide to the Symbolism, Techniques, Rituals, Sacred Texts, Psychology, Anatomy, and History of Sexuality.* Rochester, Vt.: Inner Traditions, 1991.

———. *The Yoni: Sacred Symbol of Female Creative Power.* Rochester, Vt.: Inner Traditions, 1996.

Crenshaw, Theresa L. *The Alchemy of Love and Lust: Discovering Our Sex Hormones and How They Determine Who We Love, When We Love, and How Often We Love.* New York: G. P. Putnam's Sons Publishers, 1996.

Crenshaw, Theresa L., and James P. Goldberg. *Sexual Pharmacology: Drugs That Affect Sexual Function.* New York: Norton Publishing, 1996.

Croutier, Alev Lytle. *Harem: The World Behind the Veil.* New York: Abbeville Press, 1989.

———. *Taking the Waters: Spirit, Art, Sensuality.* New York: Abbeville Press, 1992.

Dening, Sarah. *The Mythology of Sex.* New York: Simon and Schuster, 1996.

Dodson, Betty. *Sex for One: The Joy of Selfloving.* New York: Crown Publishing, 1987.

Douglas, Nik, and Penny Slinger. *Sexual Secrets: The Alchemy of Ecstasy.* New York: Destiny Books, 1979.

Frazier, Greg and Beverly. *Aphrodisiac Cookery: Ancient and Modern.* San Francisco, Calif.: Troubador Press, 1970.

Gittleman, Ann Louise. *Super Nutrition for Menopause.* New York: Pocket Books, 1993.

Gladstar, Rosemary. *Herbal Healing for Women.* New York: Fireside, 1993.

Green, James. *Male Herbal.* Freedom, Calif.: Crossing Press, 1991.

Hoffmann, David. *The New Holistic Herbal.* Shaftesbury: Element Books, 1983.

Jwala. *Sacred Sex: Ecstatic Techniques for Empowering Relationships.* Saline, Mich.: McNaughton and Gunn, 1993.

Keville, Kathi, and Mindy Green. *Aromatherapy: A Complete Guide to the Healing Art.* Freedom, Calif.: Crossing Press, 1995.

Malvern, Marjorie. *Venus in Sackcloth.* Carbondale, Ill.: Southern Illinois University Press, 1975.

Mann, A. T., and Jane Lyle. *Sacred Sexuality.* Rockport, Mass.: Element Books, 1995.

Mascetti, Manuela Dunn. *The Song of Eve.* New York: Simon and Schuster, 1990.

McIntyre, Anne. *Herbs for Mother and Child.* London: Sheldon Press, 1988.

———. *The Complete Woman's Herbal.*

London: Gaia Books, 1994.

———. *The Herbal for Pregnancy and Childbirth.* Shaftesbury: Element Books, 1992.

Riggs, Maribeth. *The Scented Bath: A Gift of Luxury from Nature's Garden.* New York: Viking Penguin Books, 1991.

Roberts, Elizabeth, and Elias Amidon. *Earth Prayers.* New York: HarperCollins, 1991.

Rose, Jeanne. *The Aromatherapy Book.* Berkeley: North Atlantic Books, 1992.

Soule, Deb. *The Roots of Healing.* New York: Citadel Press, 1995.

Walker, Barbara G. *The Women's Encyclopedia of Myths and Secrets.* New York: Harper and Row, 1983.

Walton, Alan Hull. *Aphrodisiacs: From Legend to Prescription.* Westport, Conn.: Associated Bookseller, 1958.

Watson, Cynthia Mervis. *Love Potions: A Guide to Aphrodisiacs and Sexual Pleasures.* Los Angeles, Calif.: Putnam Publishing Group, 1993.

Weed, Susun. *Breast Cancer? Breast Health!: The Wise Woman Way.* New York: Ash Tree, 1996.

———. *The Wise Woman Herbal for the Menopausal Years.* New York: Ash Tree, 1992.

Wild, Antony. *The East India Company Book of Chocolate.* London: HarperCollins, 1995.